In her insightful book, Paula guides readers through the foundations and practice of effective coaching. With relatable examples and practical resources, she emphasizes coaching as "heart work," motivating us to enhance our skills. Her comparison of coaching to a relay race highlights the importance of both theory and practice. This engaging read is essential for all coaches, from beginners to veterans, and offers invaluable reflections that resonate deeply. A true mentor, Polk inspires us to empower teachers and students alike.

—**Soo Cho**, Frisco ISD language coach

Enhancing Instruction for Multilingual Learners invites every educator into a reflective space, centering what we *can* control in the complex work of supporting multilingual learners. With compassion and clarity, Paula Polk shows us how to grow alongside our students—igniting a light within ourselves, our colleagues, and the systems we seek to transform. This book is a must-read for any teacher, coach, campus administrator, or district leader committed to improving instruction and outcomes for *all* learners.

—**Aimee Daddi**, Secondary Coordinator for Emergent Bilinguals in Plano ISD

Finally, a book dedicated to supporting language acquisition through an instructional coaching lens! This book is the perfect balance of research and practical implications, all while underscoring a universal truth: we must engage and collaborate with all stakeholders to increase student outcomes. Each chapter of the book provides foundational learning and a framework for implementation—everything from questions to pose to educators, things to reflect upon as coaches, and ways to confer with students. *Enhancing Instruction for Multilingual Learners* honors the needs of the teacher, team, and campus and offers a multitude of ways to coach for student success.

—**Curstin Ploch**, EdM, ESL coordinator

In *Enhancing Instruction for Multilingual Learners*, a focus on effective coaching practices makes this book a standout resource for instructional leaders. By offering actionable, research-driven strategies, Polk empowers coaches to guide and support educators in creating inclusive, student-centered classrooms. The emphasis on collaboration and reflective practices ensures not only that multilingual learners thrive academically and linguistically but also that educators grow professionally in the process. This is an indispensable guide for coaches committed to equity and excellence in multilingual education.

—**Nautami Patel**, language coach

In this book, Paula Polk recognizes the complexities of working from a space where the educational leader is part coach and part advocate for multilingual learners. Referencing past research as well as current educational equity and coaching greats, she writes in a way that synthesizes the information that's out there while making real, actionable recommendations that educators can put into practice immediately.

—**Lisa Morales**, ESL education coordinator

ENHANCING
INSTRUCTION FOR MULTILINGUAL LEARNERS

ENHANCING INSTRUCTION FOR MULTILINGUAL LEARNERS

Coaching Practices to Empower Students

PAULA POLK

Arlington, Virginia USA

2111 Wilson Boulevard, Suite 300 • Arlington, VA 22201 USA
Phone: 800-933-2723 or 703-578-9600
Website: www.ascd.org • Email: member@ascd.org
Author guidelines: www.ascd.org/write

Richard Culatta, *Chief Executive Officer*; Anthony Rebora, *Chief Content Officer*; Genny Ostertag, *Managing Director, Book Acquisitions & Editing*; Bill Varner, *Senior Acquisitions* Editor; Mary Beth Nielsen, *Director, Book Editing*; Megan Doyle, *Editor*; Masie Chong, *Senior Graphic Designer*; Valerie Younkin, *Senior Production Designer*; Kelly Marshall, *Production Manager*; Shajuan Martin, *E-Publishing Specialist*; Christopher Logan, *Senior Production Specialist*

Copyright © 2025 ASCD. All rights reserved. It is illegal to reproduce copies of this work in print or electronic format (including reproductions displayed on a secure intranet or stored in a retrieval system or other electronic storage device from which copies can be made or displayed) without the prior written permission of the publisher. By purchasing only authorized electronic or print editions and not participating in or encouraging piracy of copyrighted materials, you support the rights of authors and publishers. Readers who wish to reproduce or republish excerpts of this work in print or electronic format may do so for a small fee by contacting the Copyright Clearance Center (CCC), 222 Rosewood Dr., Danvers, MA 01923, USA (phone: 978-750-8400; fax: 978-646-8600; web: www.copyright.com). To inquire about site licensing options or any other reuse, contact ASCD Permissions at www.ascd.org/permissions or permission@ascd.org. For a list of vendors authorized to license ASCD ebooks to institutions, see www.ascd.org/epubs. Send translation inquiries to translations@ascd.org.

ASCD® is a registered trademark of Association for Supervision and Curriculum Development. All other trademarks contained in this book are the property of, and reserved by, their respective owners, and are used for editorial and informational purposes only. No such use should be construed to imply sponsorship or endorsement of the book by the respective owners.

All web links in this book are correct as of the publication date below but may have become inactive or otherwise modified since that time. If you notice a deactivated or changed link, please email books@ascd.org with the words "Link Update" in the subject line. In your message, please specify the web link, the book title, and the page number on which the link appears.

PAPERBACK ISBN: 978-1-4166-3373-0   ASCD product #125009 n7/25

PDF E-BOOK ISBN: 978-1-4166-3374-7; see Books in Print for other formats.

Quantity discounts are available: email programteam@ascd.org or call 800-933-2723, ext. 5773, or 703-575-5773. For desk copies, go to www.ascd.org/deskcopy.

Library of Congress Cataloging-in-Publication Data
Names: Polk, Paula author
Title: Enhancing instruction for multilingual learners : coaching practices to empower students / Paula Polk.
Description: Arlington, Virginia : ASCD, [2025] | Includes bibliographical references and index.
Identifiers: LCCN 2025010951 (print) | LCCN 2025010952 (ebook) | ISBN 9781416633730 paperback | ISBN 9781416633747 pdf
Subjects: LCSH: Language teachers—In-service training—United States | Employees—Coaching of—United States | Teaching teams—United States | English language—Study and teaching—Foreign speakers | English language—Study and teaching—United States | Multilingual education—United States | Language acquisition—United States | Inclusive education—United States
Classification: LCC P53.85 .P63 2025 (print) | LCC P53.85 (ebook) | DDC 418.0071—dc23/eng/20250519
LC record available at https://lccn.loc.gov/2025010951
LC ebook record available at https://lccn.loc.gov/2025010952

34 33 32 31 30 29 28 27 26 25   1 2 3 4 5 6 7 8 9 10 11 12

To Andre for enhancing my life in every way

To my boys, Preston and Peyton,

for empowering me to lead by example

To my mom, Vada, for being my first coach

ENHANCING INSTRUCTION FOR MULTILINGUAL LEARNERS

Introduction 1

1. Core Coaching Beliefs 7

2. Coaching for Language Proficiency 20

3. Coaching Moves 43

4. Student-Centered Coaching Models 66

5. Coaching Through Collaborative Planning 91

6. Teacher-Centered Coaching Models 108

Conclusion 136

Acknowledgments 139

Appendixes 141

References 152

Index 156

About the Author 161

Introduction

"We're building the plane as we're flying it," noted my district coordinator, Aimee. I tilted my head ever so slightly in an effort to more fully comprehend the implications. I was a brand-new language coach, a position that my district had just created. It would be my first year working outside the classroom, and I was eager to make an impact. I spent much of the previous summer reading, researching, and wondering—about instructional coaching, about multilingual learners, about instruction and leadership. What would each day look like? How would I divide my time between two assigned campuses with two very different demographics? How would I get people to trust me in a new role, one that had never existed before? What exactly *was* my role anyway? Oh, and by the way, where might one find that fully built plane?

Aimee elaborated, "Yes, we're building the plane as we're flying it. We're doing something new that hasn't been done before. Our previous model only widened the achievement gap. This new model is a step toward partnering with all stakeholders to grow our English learners. They deserve it." She was right. Multilingual learners deserve opportunities to benefit from the expertise of all stakeholders on campus. In that moment, I began to fully realize the pioneering nature of the work we were doing.

Instructional coaching has taken the education field by storm. Born out of adult learning theory, the idea has gained traction because it works. Humans are social learners. For much of human history, apprenticeships were the primary means of learning a skill or trade. Apprenticeships enabled the apprentice to learn alongside someone, to receive job-embedded professional learning in their craft. As Atul

Gawande has pointed out, "Coaching done well may be the most effective intervention designed for human performance." This quote, often cited by instructional coaching expert Jim Knight (2017, p. 2), makes a case for apprenticeship and coaching.

The fact is, our educational climate is rife with teacher burnout and shortages; teachers often feel neither honored nor respected. Coaching, by design, honors the fact that educators are thinking professionals. Rather than traditional professional development that says, "Sit there and let me show you what you don't know," coaching as professional learning asks, "May I work alongside you so we can discover new ways of facilitating student learning together?"

Although instructional coaching has gained footing in schools across the United States, particularly in math and literacy, the idea of coaching for language acquisition is a new phenomenon. The passing of the Equal Education Opportunities Act (EEOA) of 1974 led districts across the country "to take appropriate action to overcome language barriers that impede equal participation by its students in its instructional programs" (U.S. Department of Justice, 2021). In practice, this meant allocating professional staff to serve students whose first language is not English. Such staff includes English as a second language (ESL) teachers, as well as teachers and specialists in English for speakers of other languages (ESOL). Traditionally, these educators have been responsible for testing students' language levels, getting students settled in their English immersion classroom, and pulling them from class to provide instruction in English language development. This segregated instructional model has remained in place for decades to fulfill state and federal compliance requirements to provide students with educational opportunities to help them become bilingual or even multilingual.

It's been 50 years since the Equal Education Opportunities Act was passed. Our world has since become a more global community and the United States has become more diverse; our school populations now reflect the beauty of this cultural and linguistic diversity. Yet the question remains, Do our instructional practices for multilingual learners honor these changes? In many schools, the resounding answer is "no." Antiquated practices of "pull out," in which one professional is solely responsible for the language proficiency of multilingual learners, no longer suffice, if they ever did.

If we want to serve all students equitably, developing an innovative mindset that brings all stakeholders to the table on behalf of multilingual learners is key. In this age of professional learning communities, districts and schools must move away from the practice of having one professional educator bear the sole responsibility for an entire demographic. A shift toward equity and inclusion cannot occur in isolation. It requires partnership among all stakeholders.

Moving toward an inclusive practice means honoring the research regarding language acquisition practices. Coaching for language acquisition and proficiency combines

- A commitment to advocacy.
- Research-based language acquisition methods.
- Principles from instructional coaching and adult learning.

Such coaching requires an instructional leader or coach who personifies partnership while deliberately nudging practitioners toward targeted instruction.

To coach for language acquisition, we must understand what comprises quality Tier 1 instruction, believe in the power of collaboration, and be determined to advocate for multilingual students whose presence can be perceived as a burden by some and an afterthought by others. In many cases, when we coach for the benefit of multilingual students, we're acting as agents of change, slowly shifting mindsets through deliberate interactions. Coaching from this lens is a journey that affects the coach just as much as those coached.

Charting the Course

It's my hope to take you on a journey that focuses on coaching for multilingual students' success. I have engaged in this work as a practitioner, an instructional leader, and a systems-level facilitator. I am still joyfully on this journey as a lifelong learner, and I invite you to join me. In the chapters that follow, we'll look at the foundations of coaching, at equity, and at the intricacies of growing English language proficiency.

Chapter 1 outlines *core coaching beliefs* that instructional leaders should embrace in partnering with educators. The overarching core beliefs of motivation, mindset, and moves provide a foundation for stakeholders to advocate for the academic success of multilingual learners. Each belief is undergirded with corresponding actions and commitments to emotional intelligence, collective efficacy, continuous improvement, lifelong learning, partnership, and communication. By unpacking how each of these beliefs and commitments creates an environment for coaching, we're able to enter into the work knowing, as Brené Brown (2018) would say, it's about people, people, people.

Chapter 2 defines beliefs about language acquisition and highlights the *layers of quality language acquisition instruction* essential for multilingual students' success. The chapter will analyze resources that facilitate instruction that is scaffolded to the proficiency levels of multilingual students. By detailing how instructional leaders can leverage language acquisition strategies to partner with teachers, we promote learning opportunities that are conducive to multilingual learners' acquisition of social and academic English. We begin by noting the importance of developing an asset-based mindset to establish an equitable foundation for learning, and we provide practical examples that show how to create language- and literacy-rich environments. We will round out our learning by unpacking the elements of linguistically accommodated instruction that grows language proficiency.

Chapter 3 combines the concepts addressed in Chapters 1 and 2—core coaching beliefs and layers of quality language acquisition instruction—to discuss appropriate *coaching moves* that instructional leaders can make, based on their rapport with the teacher and the linguistic and academic needs of the student. We look at three different levels of coaching—consultative, reflective, and collaborative coaching. Each has several moves an instructional leader can make to build teacher capacity.

Chapter 4 focuses on two *student-centered coaching models*—Student Goal Setting and Inclusion with a Purpose. Instructional leaders will learn how to take students through a goal-setting process that enables them to monitor their own linguistic progress and use the goal-setting cycle with embedded inclusion support to serve the needs of multilingual learners. Opportunities to use coaching moves that build teacher knowledge of linguistic strategies are woven throughout the discussion.

Chapter 5 focuses on *coaching through collaborative planning* as a prerequisite for quality instruction. To access content at higher levels, multilingual students need instruction that is scaffolded according to their language proficiency. This can only happen with intentionality during the time that teachers plan instruction. This chapter provides guiding questions and coaching moves that will enable an instructional leader to engage in collaborative planning with content teachers to enhance linguistic richness and engagement during instruction.

Chapter 6 looks at two *teacher-centered coaching models* that coaches, administrators, and teacher leaders can use to enhance their expertise: Coaching Minicycles and Co-Teaching Cycles. We define each model and unpack practical coaching moves that focus on teacher practice—specifically on linguistically scaffolded instructional moves.

Each chapter concludes with a Mind Your Ms box, which crystalizes how, in the context of that chapter, you can maximize your motivation, mold your mindset with solid research, and make appropriate moves.

Our journey will begin with establishing the core beliefs that guide our coaching work. Core beliefs are to coaching what rules and procedures are to the classroom—they help us lay a foundation for learning and change.

1

Core Coaching Beliefs

There are many ideologies surrounding instructional coaching. These include the groundbreaking work of Jim Knight and the instructional coaching group, Elena Aguilar and the Bright Morning Team's transformational coaching, and Diane Sweeney's student-centered coaching. As I embarked on my transition from classroom practitioner into coaching, each of these authors came to be faces on my Mount Rushmore of Coaching. Each framework brought a unique perspective that helped to connect the dots of what it meant to strategically build the capacity of fellow educators.

When I began my journey as a language coach, it seemed to meld two roles: that of a traditional ESL teacher and the emerging role of an instructional coach. How could two traditionally unrelated roles merge to have an actionable effect on a campus? How could I combine the work of a teacher devoted to the language development of multilingual learners with that of an instructional coach? To answer these questions, I synthesized the beliefs and best practices around teaching multilingual learners with the work of the coaching pioneers I studied. This synthesis formed the basis for my core beliefs about coaching. By pairing those beliefs with research-based language acquisition methodologies, I found I could partner with teachers to positively affect learning for multilingual learners.

It Begins with Self-Awareness

"Coaching is people work." This statement, made by my own coaching mentor Laurea Myers, often plays in a loop in my head, particularly when I'm facing a coaching challenge. Her words describe a coach and their work—someone devoted to the success of others. Being able to serve others comes only with a great deal of self-awareness and internal work. Awareness of our own interpersonal or "soft" skills informs our style of coaching and how we show up as a coach with our coachees. For example, if I know I'm prone to thinking about how I'll respond while others are speaking, I can paraphrase to hold myself accountable for committed listening. However, the only way that I know to hold myself accountable is if I'm first aware of my own communication skills. Self-awareness is the foundation of coaching because without it, we can't successfully do "people work."

As we work with others, the interactions, conversations, conflicts, and experiences we have with them lend themselves to moments of self-awareness. Planning with a team of teachers who have a tendency to veer off topic and therefore develop minimal plans might make me realize how much I value decision making and efficiency. Conversations with a teacher who begins every interaction asking me for a favor rather than asking how I'm doing might make me notice that personal connection is important to me. Our everyday work with others can provide moments of clarity around our core values.

It's crucial, therefore, to intentionally engage in developing self-awareness. My self-awareness journey involved lots of reading, journaling, and reflecting. Practicing self-awareness through interactions with teachers, coaches, principals, and administrators formed my core beliefs about coaching. Of course, one need not have the title of coach to coach. A principal, for instance, can choose to lead a building using a coaching style to develop educators rather than simply "managing" them. A classroom teacher often coaches students and fellow teachers by providing feedback and asking questions, key communication moves of coaching.

Six core beliefs should undergird our coaching; these fall under the categories of motivation, mindset, and moves (see Figure 1.1). What should motivate our coaching work? What mindset should a coach have? What moves make for effective coaching?

FIGURE 1.1
Core Coaching Beliefs

Motivation	Mindset	Moves
Emotional Intelligence I believe in order to coach others, you must actively cultivate emotional intelligence.	**Lifelong Learning** I believe a coach continually seeks out opportunities to be a learner.	**Partnership** I believe a coach engages stakeholders as partners.
Collective Efficacy I believe in order to coach others, you must believe in their ability to grow their instructional practice.	**Continuous Improvement** I believe a coach must have a commitment to improving their practice.	**Communication** I believe a coach uses communication skills as a vehicle to partner for professional learning.

Motivation

Motivation is the willingness to do something or is something that causes such willingness. This definition strikes at the heart of coaching. Motivation is our "why." Why did you become a coach or decide to lead from a coaching lens? Why is the success of multilingual learners important to you? It might be helpful to journal your answer to these questions, another step in the journey of self-awareness.

Core Belief 1. Emotional Intelligence

At the start of my coaching journey, I developed my coaching vision as I read *The Art of Coaching: Effective Strategies for School Transformation* by Elena Aguilar (2013). She writes, "When I question why I'm doing what I'm doing or when I feel unmoored by the challenges in my daily practice, I return to my vision" (p. 29). I took her advice to heart and developed my own vision for coaching. I have returned to that vision many times, and it has evolved as I have grown in my self-awareness as a coach and person. My very first coaching vision reads as follows:

I coach to empower educators to feel competent and passionate about their impact on students and colleagues. I coach to enhance educational outcomes for children from all walks of life.

As you develop your coaching vision, you might find that it includes others—and that's because coaching is people work. Our willingness or motivation to coach reaches farther than our own needs. It stretches our minds, hearts, and hands, enabling us to see, feel, and touch others' needs. Motivation is the "heart work."

At the center of this heart work is the cultivation of emotional intelligence. Peter Salovey and John D. Mayer defined emotional intelligence as "an ability to monitor one's own and others' emotions, to discriminate among them, and to use the information to guide one's thinking and actions" (Brackett et al., 2025). The verbs in this definition leap off the page. *Monitor. Discriminate. Guide.* An emotionally intelligent individual is adept at monitoring emotions as data to guide their mindsets and moves. Coaching is collaborative: an instructional leader or coach co-labors with a teacher for the academic success of students. Nothing can sabotage a collaborative endeavor faster than an inability to navigate one's emotions or those of others. Conversely, nothing can nurture a collaborative endeavor more effectively than navigating emotions wisely. Yet developing emotional intelligence requires reflection and vulnerability, first with oneself and then with others—and they both require a willingness to be courageous and to connect emotionally with others as we do the "people work."

My first year as a 3rd grade teacher was a huge transition for me. I had taught 1st grade for nine years in two different school districts. Literacy was my passion. I knew no greater joy than giving the gift of literacy to students before they left my care at the end of the year. But after nine years teaching the same grade level, opening a campus in a new district and leading a grade-level team, I was ready for a change. I aspired to lead and coach in some way, so I needed to challenge myself. I branched out to teach a new grade—3rd grade—as well as a new subject—math. First grade math, piece of cake, but 3rd grade math? In a state standardized testing grade? Teaching two sections? Although it terrified me, the challenge excited me.

At the start of the school year, I shared my fears with Michelle, my assistant principal, who would also be my evaluator. The first time she came into observe, she came unannounced, which I preferred because I don't enjoy the pomp and pageantry that can be associated with scheduled evaluations. She watched, listened, chatted with students, and took notes on her laptop. She left, and my day continued. I taught my switch class in math and science, scarfing down a 20-minute lunch while checking emails, and then I went on to do recess duty, lesson plan during my planning period, repeat math and science with my homeroom, and finally carpool duty.

When I walked into the front office to check my mailbox, I found this handwritten note from Michelle:

> Paula,
>
> Thank you for allowing me to visit your class. I noticed so many routines and structures in place to support student autonomy and success. I took pictures so I can share ideas with staff of visuals that would be helpful.

I could feel my lips curving up into a smile and my shoulders releasing as the stress of a long day began to melt. This note, which I still have tucked away in the "smile file" drawer of my home office, was a bid for emotional connection.

Jim Knight (2015) calls this being a "witness to the good." In *Better Conversations*, he writes, "Too often, the challenges of being an educator and the emotional exhaustion that comes with trying to reach every child every day make it difficult for teachers to fully comprehend the good they are doing" (p. 117). This is exactly what I felt as I headed back from carpool that day: the emotional and mental weight that comes with being "on" all day as a teacher. Knight encourages us to communicate to people the positive things we see. Witnessing the good is a service we provide to those we coach. Coaching is *seeing* people. When we cultivate emotional intelligence, we make a habit of seeing people.

Core Belief 2. Collective Efficacy

To grow their instructional practice, a coach must believe in the ability of those they coach. Psychologist Albert Bandura (1997) coined the term *collective efficacy*, which he defines as "a group's shared belief in its conjoint capability to organize and execute the courses of action required to produce given levels of attainment" (p. 477). Simply stated, it's a group's confidence in their ability to get results. Educational researcher John Hattie (Waack, 2018) identifies collective teacher efficacy (CTE) as the influence with the greatest effect size, at 1.52. That's greater than Response to Intervention (1.29), planning (.76), feedback (.70), and even teacher-student relationships (.52). The collective belief of a faculty in their ability to positively affect students has more influence, then, than any other factor. Hattie explains that the purpose of CTE is to build each teacher's efficacy through *collaborative conversations based on evidence collected*. This makes my coaching heart shout "Amen!" Why? Because coaching is all about creating a collaborative partnership to build teacher capacity through conversations rooted in data, artifacts, and evidence.

If a coach doesn't believe in the coachee's ability to grow and improve their practice, any coaching efforts will be in vain. No one can learn with you if you make them feel small. We have deeply internalized this with our students, evidenced by the mantra "Kids don't care how much you know until they know how much you *care*." Similarly, adult learners need to have their knowledge and experiences validated (Aguilar & Cohen, 2022). This unconditional positive regard enables us to coach the expert educator who seems to need nothing in the way of coaching, the novice teacher who is overwhelmed with the often-jarring transition from theory to practice, as well as the burned-out teacher who has nary a positive comment to offer. We can coach in the best of times and the worst of times because we believe not just in the power of coaching, but in the goodness of those who entered into a profession that requires a servant's heart. We choose to believe and demonstrate belief in our fellow educators' ability to grow their instructional pedagogy and practice. As a coach, we must be willing to cultivate our own emotional intelligence and our belief in the capabilities of those we seek to coach. If we seek to inspire change, we must first believe it's possible.

Mindset

Mindset is a person's way of thinking. In the framework of the core coaching beliefs, mindset represents the "head" of coaching—how we engage our minds in the work we do as coaches. We exert mental labor as we plan conversations and learning experiences with those we coach.

Core Belief 3. Continuous Improvement

To coach others, we need to commit to continuous personal improvement. Humans are continually changing, with both age and life experience, whether that change is the loss of a loved one, a marriage, an expanding family, or a global pandemic. These often lead us to new discoveries about ourselves. Committing to continuous personal improvement as a coach means actively reflecting, seeking feedback, and setting goals based on that reflection and feedback.

As my first year as a language coach came to a close, I thought ahead to the following year. I pondered all the things I wanted to do differently, do better. What went well? Was I successful? How did I define success in this role? As I looked back, I realized I wasn't able to precisely name my successes, and that left me feeling defeated. As a 1st grade teacher, my measure of success was how many students left me able to read. As a 3rd grade teacher, my measure of success was how independent my learners were by the end of the year and how they performed on standardized assessments.

But what was success as a coach? Was it how many teachers reached out to me or how much trust my principal had in me? Was it how many teachers I worked with or how much of an increase I saw in their students' performance? More specifically as a language acquisition coach, was it raised awareness on how to serve multilingual learners? The teachers' level of comfort in teaching linguistically diverse students? Whether and by how much their students' proficiency increased on the state language assessment? Better still, was it how celebrated and welcomed diverse families felt in our school community?

Perhaps it was a little bit of each. Once again, I had more questions than answers, a recurring theme in my first year as a coach. I have learned that the abundance of questions and, more important, the act of questioning oneself are indicators of self-awareness, exemplifying a commitment to continuous improvement. The very acts of continually reflecting, soliciting feedback, and questioning ourselves are proof that we're focused on improving ourselves.

Core Belief 4. Lifelong Learning

Coaches are often the developers and deliverers of professional learning. Understanding adult learning theory, instructional design, and the principles of engaging facilitation ensure that what we deliver honors teachers as thinking professionals. Professional learning is all about impact; the learner should leave the experience changed in some way (Aguilar & Cohen, 2022), more curious, inspired, or challenged.

A coach's personal commitment to never stop learning empowers them to be a conduit of learning for those they coach both informally and formally.

Coaches can provide learning experiences in a variety of formats, from modeling a lesson to creating a digital learning playlist. However, because a coach is continually pouring *out* knowledge, it's imperative that knowledge pours *in*. "He who seeks to teach must never cease to learn." This quote was my email signature as a brand-new teacher; the more experience I gain as an educator, the more I see its truth. We can't pour from an empty cup, and if we try, we won't show up as the best version of ourselves.

A coach must continually seek out opportunities to develop their practice. In a post-pandemic world in which videoconferencing has become the norm, we now have access to more on-demand professional learning than ever before. Using your social media of choice to develop a professional learning network can unlock the door to a wide range of learning. Podcasts, webinars, newsletters from field experts, books, and even resources shared through online posts provide a multiplicity of free opportunities where you can learn, grow, and develop your expertise.

In my first year of coaching, I lamented to a veteran coach, "I'm taking books home each night to try to read and learn more about my role, but I don't have time once I'm home!" With school-age children and a commitment to work-life balance, I just couldn't get to the reading. "Why don't you just build time into your schedule here at school to read?" my coach suggested. "Read here?" I asked, surprised. "But shouldn't I be coaching?" "Learning how to coach *is* coaching," she replied.

Cue the light bulb! Taking time to pour into ourselves shows that we take coaching seriously. From that day on, my schedule reflected my values. I set aside 30 minutes each week to devote to professional reading or research because I simply can't give to others what I don't have.

A coaching mindset means we're committed to improving our practice as coaches through self-reflection, feedback, and questioning. It means we seek out professional learning opportunities and grow our professional learning network. We fully engage our minds because we desire to teach, and so we must never cease to learn.

Moves

The *Cambridge Dictionary* defines *moves* in this way: "to (cause to) progress, change, or happen in a particular way or direction." Moves are the hands of coaching; they describe the larger actions that underlie all of our smaller coaching moves.

The concept of partnership underlies the work of a coach. To build the capacity of teachers, a coach must engage *as a full partner*, understanding that they have as much to learn from the teacher as the teacher has to learn from them. The idea of partnering is key when engaging adult learners. American educator Matthew Knowles's principles of adult learning (Instructional Design Australia, 2024; Lee, 2024) tell us that adults

- Need to know why they're learning something.
- Learn by doing, thereby needing to be involved in their learning.
- Thrive in problem-centered learning.
- Prefer learning that is relevant and of immediate use.

Core Belief 5. Partnership

When we take a partnership approach to coaching, we link arms with teachers and engage in the work. When we confer with teachers about the needs of multilingual learners, we can advocate for learners *and* explain the purpose of implementing particular linguistic scaffolds. In later chapters, we will explore coaching models, such as Co-Teaching Cycles and Inclusion with a Purpose. These models are grounded in partnership. When we enter into the Co-Teaching Cycle, we experiment with literacy-rich strategies that increase the engagement and English language development of multilingual learners. As we set goals for Inclusion with a Purpose, we act as a guide on the side, modeling linguistic strategies that are of immediate use to teachers. In each type of coaching model, we create spaces for both the coach and teacher *as partners* to reflect on teaching and learning. By doing so, we honor teacher choice and voice. We consider it a privilege to be invited into a teacher's classroom, one we maintain by grounding our coaching work in partnership.

Core Belief 6. Communication

A coach uses communication skills to partner for professional learning. In *RESULTS Coaching*, author Kathy Kee and her team (2010) write, "Language is the essential connector, and how we choose to use it will significantly impact the relationships and identities of those we lead" (p. 71). To achieve such an effect, we must be conscientious of our communications skills. Lev Vygotsky, who invariably appears in undergraduate Introduction to Education courses, suggests that social interaction is crucial to our cognitive development. We're social learners. Further, a key principle of partnership is dialogue. Fostering dialogue enables coaches to set themselves up as thinking partners, balancing inquiry with advocacy and making it easier for the coachee to feel seen and safe to share what they think (Knight, 2015).

Communication that changes instructional practices is rooted in the conviction that coaching conversations are entered into with positive intent, built on mutual respect, and sustained with optimism. The number of students with the gift of multilingualism continues to increase across the United States. This is a gift—but also a challenge that can feel daunting to teachers and cause feelings of inadequacy and frustration. To successfully navigate this situation in our current political and educational climate, coaches and leaders need to use communication skills with intention. Coaches focused on language acquisition must study, practice, and apply the skills of listening, paraphrasing, and questioning, a reflection of their positive intent.

In my second year of language coaching, we saw an increase in immigrant students who had no previous exposure to the English language. This surprised many teachers. A few months after school started, I received an email from our office staff letting me know that a student from Hong Kong had enrolled and would begin after the upcoming weekend. The staff member informed me that the dad spoke some English and had communicated that his 5th grade son spoke a bit of English as well. I spent time that week preparing a newcomer kit for the student and teacher. I had found that offering a visual schedule that featured translated words, basic needs cards with visuals and labels in the native language, and a calming fidget went a long way to help newcomers transition into their new U.S. classroom. I also added a one-pager for teachers with quick tips for serving newcomers, as well as a greeting in the student's native language.

I then set up a meeting with Mrs. Sparks, the 5th grade teacher. Her current multilingual students had mastered basic social English but still needed to work on their academic English. She had yet to have a student at the beginning level of language proficiency, a situation that many teachers across our district were now experiencing.

I prepared myself for our conversation. I played out questions she might ask and answers I might give; I reminded myself of what a gifted writing teacher Mrs. Sparks was and how she always had innovative ideas for her team. I tried to imagine what concerns she might have and why she might have them. I reminded myself of a lesson I learned about myself the previous year: don't dive right into the conversation; instead, connect first. I needed to make sure to ask her about the new addition to her family, a new grandbaby, her first.

"So, he doesn't speak any English at all?" she asked with knitted brows. I nodded. "Goodness. We have a test on Friday. What's he supposed to do? Will you just pull him out? I've never had one this new."

I took in Mrs. Sparks's words and nervous energy and leaned into the partnership with my response. "I made a visual schedule for the student and a few basic needs cards with Mandarin and English phrases. I'll spend some time here in the morning with you on his first day. What else will we need to make the transition smoother?" I wanted to communicate to her that she was not alone, that we were a team, and that she wasn't expected to figure this out by herself. I also wanted to honor her autonomy and knowledge. Although she may not have been the language acquisition expert, she was an expert in her classroom, and we could be thinking partners. Neither of us had all the answers, but together we could come up with answers that would enable both her and the student to adjust to this transition.

"Oh, you being here in the morning will be great... just in case." Although I knew there would be other challenges ahead, that moment taught me the power of preparing for a coaching conversation and using it as a vehicle to partner with teachers for the success of students.

Leveraging effective communication as a vehicle for partnership enhances our own coaching practice, as well as the instructional practice of the teachers we coach. When we fully employ coaching moves with a belief in partnership, we don't just talk the talk, but we link arms with teachers and walk the walk.

Tying It Up

In this chapter, we have explored the core coaching beliefs that will sustain the work of a language coach. These beliefs serve as the heart, head, and hands of coaching, enabling us to engage all stakeholders for the success of multilingual students. When we actively cultivate emotional intelligence and practice a belief in collective efficacy, we maximize our ability to motivate ourselves and those we serve. By looking to continuously improve and by seeking out professional learning, we demonstrate a commitment to molding our mindset. Using sound communication as a vehicle to engage in full partnership, we make the moves that build teacher capacity for student achievement.

Mind Your Ms

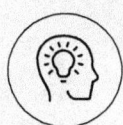

Maximize Your Motivation
- Consider why you became a coach and what drives your desire, then write down your own coaching vision.
- Frame success: When you look forward to the last day of school, how do you want to feel? Take a moment to journal your hopes and dreams.

Mold Your Mindset

Research and read about various coaching frameworks to build your knowledge of instructional coaching. Here are some suggestions:
- *The Art of Coaching: Effective Strategies for School Transformation* (2013) by Elena Aguilar
- *Better Conversations: Coaching Ourselves and Each Other to Be More Credible, Caring, and Connected* (2015) by Jim Knight
- *RESULTS Coaching: The New Essential for School Leaders* (2010) by Kathy Kee and colleagues

Make Your Moves
- Assess your communication skills using the tools found in Appendix A, Self-Rating Tools A–C.
- Consider keeping a journal to record your thoughts, noticings, and wonderings before or after coaching conversations and interactions.

2

Coaching for Language Proficiency

My first year of language coaching felt like a whirlwind. As a classroom teacher, I taught many linguistically diverse students each year, but this was different. Now I was supporting multilingual students, their families, *and* their teachers. Between the jargon of language acquisition and the terminology associated with legal compliance tasks, I often felt like *I* was learning a new language.

To begin with, let's consider some terms associated with multilingual learners. (See Appendix B, Terms for Students and Programs.) The term *multilingual* has many implications, both positive and negative, evolving from the deficit-based term of *limited English speaking ability* (LESA) in 1968 to *English learner* (EL) in current literature and resources from the U.S. Department of Education (Garcia, 2021). In this book, I'll use the terms *multilingual learners*, *multilingual students*, and *culturally and linguistically diverse students*:

- Multilingual learners: Students who have exposure to two or more languages and
  - Who are legally receiving English language development services, or
  - Whose parents or guardians have denied services.

- Multilingual students: Students who have exposure to two or more languages and
  - Who didn't need or qualify for English language development services due to scoring proficient on initial language placement tests.
  - Who no longer receive English language development services and have been reclassified as English proficient after meeting legal requirements.
  - Who speak an additional language or languages in the home, although their parents or guardians didn't report this fact.
- Culturally and linguistically diverse students: This includes the two groups above, as well as students who have exposure to two or more languages or dialects and
  - Whose parents or guardians didn't report additional languages either to avoid perceived labels or because of language barriers during the registration process.
  - Who are unable to report additional dialects other than Standard American English because those dialects are not yet recognized as linguistically diverse (for example, African American English or Appalachian English).

Layers of Quality Language Acquisition Instruction

Figure 2.1 presents a compilation of mindsets, practices, and strategies that must be in place for multilingual learners to receive high-quality instruction across the content areas. How does this graphic support your beliefs and practices as an instructional leader? Which words resonate most? Which words resonate least?

When taking in new information for professional learning, I find it helpful to determine what aligns with what I already believe and practice, what I call my "brain boxes." As I read and attend webinars and conference sessions, I place new terms, ideas, and strategies in those boxes. This enables me to celebrate the work I'm already doing while growing my beliefs and practices. As we work our way through this chapter, I encourage you to consider your brain boxes. Take time to celebrate the work that affirms your current practices, consider how to adjust those practices, and slowly embed new ones that increase the quality of instruction for multilingual learners.

Much like the core coaching beliefs that we discussed in Chapter 1, language acquisition instruction focuses on motivation, mindset, and moves. A language- and literacy-rich environment and linguistically accommodated instruction are the moves that support asset-based beliefs and equity-driven practices. And these latter reflect the mindset and motivation behind instruction. Our ultimate goal and responsibility toward multilingual learners is to "facilitate their transition out of programs and services within a reasonable amount of time" (U.S. Department of Justice & U.S. Department of Education, 2015). This is also known as *reclassifying students as English proficient*; we're best able to do this when all the layers are in place. Let's unpack each layer to develop a common understanding.

FIGURE 2.1

Layers of Quality Language Acquisition Instruction

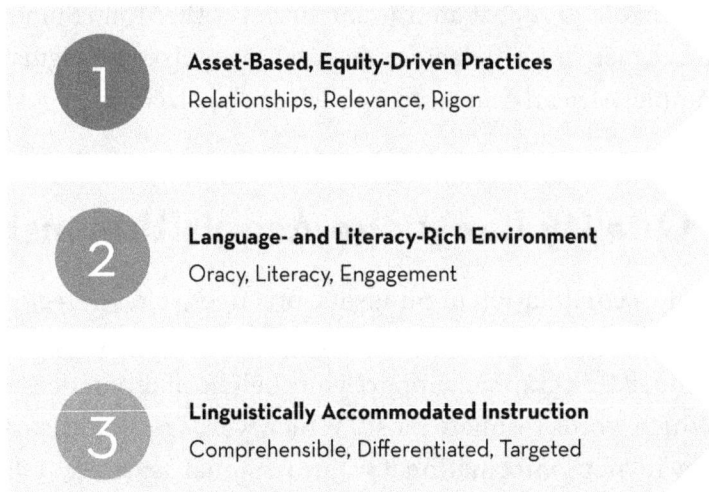

Layer 1. Asset-Based and Equity-Driven Practices

Asset-based beliefs acknowledge the funds of knowledge that all students bring to the classroom. We see evidence of these beliefs when we advocate for and speak about students in ways that highlight their assets. In contrast, a deficit mindset focuses on the skills or, in the case of multilingual learners, the language they have not yet acquired. A deficit mindset may lead educators and policymakers to blame students or their families for any perceived lack of academic success or view home languages and cultures as hindrances to overcome rather than as gifts to treasure (Snyder & Fenner, 2021). Figure 2.2 compares the two mindsets.

FIGURE 2.2

Asset-Based Mindset Versus Deficit-Based Mindset

Asset-Based Mindset	Deficit-Based Mindset
• Focuses on the strengths students bring to the learning community • Believes all students bring "funds of knowledge" to the classroom • Recognizes the unique ways culturally and linguistically diverse families contribute to the student's education • Views diversity as a positive asset • Values students' culture and language as a springboard for future success • Allows multiple entry points to honor students' cultural and linguistic backgrounds • Often looks for ways to adapt or change the system to meet student needs	• Focuses on what students lack or are unable to do • Believes students have little prior knowledge and are blank slates the teacher must fill • Overlooks the unique ways families may contribute to the student's education, particularly if they don't match the teacher's own educational background or culture • Focuses on the need or "problem" • Often leads to assumptions about what students can and can't do • Often requires the student to change to fit into the system

Equity-driven practices grow from an asset-based mindset. As often attributed to Maya Angelou, "When we know better, we can do better." Asset-based beliefs are the "knowing better," whereas equity-driven practices are the "doing better."

The first step is to evaluate our own mindset. How do we speak about our students when they don't perform well? When concerns arise about students academically, socially, or behaviorally, what do the conversations sound like? When we receive a new student who doesn't yet speak English, what is our top concern? Does our speech exude empathy for the student embarking into a new culture and system of schooling, or does it reek of annoyance with the student's lack of English?

The apprehension some teachers feel at having newcomers at the beginning level of language proficiency is often rooted in fear—fear that they won't be able to meet the student's needs. On one hand, this reveals the teacher's desire to reach their students, but on the other, it speaks to a fixed mindset that sees challenges as a threat. The truth we focus on determines whether or not our mindset leads to equity-driven practices. As coaches and instructional leaders, our truth should be honoring our commitment to continuous improvement. We do so by partnering with teachers to cultivate asset-based beliefs that lead to equitable outcomes for all students, particularly our multilingual learners.

Relationships

We noted earlier that "Children don't care how much you know until they know how much you care." This quote, often attributed to John Maxwell, has special significance in education because we cannot realize our goal of teaching and learning apart from building relationships with our students. Rita Pierson (2013) stated it plainly in her TED Talk: "Kids don't learn from people they don't like." The reverse, unfortunately, is also true; teachers can't teach students *they* don't like. Students who are unruly or disrespectful or who display unsafe behavior can easily impede a teacher's ability and desire to teach. Or a teacher may develop negative feelings about a student simply because of a clash of personalities. In such cases, students may receive a lower quality of education, a subtle opening for injustice to creep in.

James Ford wrote, "Our first job as teachers is to make sure we learn our students, that we connect with them on a real level, showing respect for their culture and affirming their worthiness to receive the best education possible" (Sparks, 2024). Which phrase resonates most with you? For me it's "affirming their worthiness." That phrase calls me up, calls *us* up. As educators, we have the ability and the responsibility to affirm the worthiness of our students. We also have the ability to deny their worthiness. This is a truth we don't ponder often enough—that the decisions we make in our classrooms, schools, and districts have implications for a person's life. As educational consultant and author Zaretta Hammond (2014) put it, "Affirmation simply means that we acknowledge the personhood of our students" (p. 76). Kids are people, too! The time teachers take to learn and connect with their students and show respect for their culture affirms their worthiness. School leaders who stand up for this core value are central to a school climate that upholds asset-based beliefs and equity-driven practices.

Once we recognize and take time to value the cultural differences our students bring to our learning community, we can begin to leverage those differences as "windows" and "mirrors" throughout the curriculum and instruction we implement. The cultural perspectives our multilingual students bring can be a window for ourselves and other students to learn about our world as global citizens. They also serve as powerful mirrors in which culturally and linguistically diverse students see their own lived experiences reflected in the classroom. When we choose books, images, and materials that represent the entire school community, we show that we value diversity and believe that everyone benefits from varied viewpoints and experiences (Snyder & Fenner, 2021).

Relevance

Relevance means empowering multilingual learners to become independent learners by meeting their affective, linguistic, and cognitive needs. *Empower* means to give someone freedom to do something. We see this in an environment in which a coach can come alongside any stakeholder and empower them to see and meet the unique needs of multilingual learners. Meeting those student needs *with relevance* happens when we attend to the learning environment and ensure high levels of engagement.

"All learners have to connect new content to what they already know. What we already know is organized according to our cultural experiences, values, and concepts" (Hammond, 2014, p. 49). Similar to the teacher brain boxes mentioned earlier, students' brain boxes are largely based on their previous experiences. Creating a relevant environment means students can easily connect their funds of knowledge to the curriculum, materials, and experiences. These must include windows, mirrors—and sliding glass doors. Rudine Sims Bishop, the mother of multicultural children's literature, famously wrote,

> Books are sometimes windows, offering views of worlds that may be real or imagined, familiar or strange. These windows are also sliding glass doors, and readers have only to walk through in imagination to become part of whatever world has been created and recreated by the author. (cited in Chenoweth, 2019)

When students see themselves and their experience while learning, it increases their sense of belonging and engagement. When students learn about others' experiences—experiences that may greatly differ from their own—it fosters empathy, perspective taking, and critical thinking.

Our aim is to empower multilingual students to be active participants in the learning process. Hammond (2014) reminds us that we can identify independent learners by how well they attend to their own learning. Educators honor this aim when we create culturally relevant and engaging environments.

Rigor

High expectations are foundational to rigor. It's imperative that we believe in the ability of multilingual students to acquire English and become independent learners. We can hold students to rigorous standards, even in the early stages of learning English. And just because a student doesn't know English doesn't mean they don't have a wealth of knowledge in their own language. I provide this caution because English speakers may be unaware that students have an abundance of content knowledge that they're able to express expertly in their native tongue. The fact is, many Americans operate in a monolingual bias. In many places across the world, speaking multiple languages is the norm. Not so in the United States, where the majority of people are monolingual.

During my first year as a language coach, I had a 5th grade student I'll call Min Joon, who had extensive knowledge of science, particularly about ocean animals. He wrote a nonfiction essay about electric eels in Korean. We worked together with scaffolds, such as sentence frames, translation tools, and word banks, to construct his essay in English. He was able to share so much information! The amount of background knowledge he possessed impressed both his classroom teachers and me. However, we shouldn't have been so surprised. This was my first confrontation with my own monolingual bias. It helped me realize that I held an incorrect belief that students needed to know English for me to teach them. I learned that to reach students, I needed to find the balance between supporting them through linguistic scaffolds and challenging them with an engaging and rigorous lesson.

Layer 2. Language- and Literacy-Rich Environment

Once we have built a foundation of asset-based beliefs that lead to equity-driven practices, we can turn our attention to the instructional moves that support multilingual students' acquisition of English. The second layer to quality language acquisition instruction is a language- and literacy-rich environment.

Language and literacy are foundational to our education system. Biologically and historically speaking, literacy is a new phenomenon. Literacy expert Louisa Moats (2020) writes, "Our brains are not as fully evolved for processing written language as they are for processing spoken language, and therefore, learning to read and write is more challenging than learning to speak" (p. 7).

Understanding the complexity of literacy and its interconnectedness with language is essential when supporting the language acquisition of multilingual students. In addition, English is a more complicated alphabetic language due to its complex spelling system and variety of dialects (Moats, 2020). Effective educators of multilingual students, whether they are coaches, administrators, or other stakeholders, should have foundational language and literacy knowledge, an appreciation of the unnaturalness of learning to read or write in any language, as well as the complexity of the English language in particular.

Let's now take a closer look at the components of language- and literacy-rich environments.

Oracy

The goal of oracy is self-expression and the exchange of information and ideas. In terms of English language acquisition, there are four domains or skills that describe how we interact with language: listening, speaking, reading, and writing (Kongsvik, n.d.). Oracy focuses on the language domains of *listening and speaking*.

Listening is a receptive skill that requires the listener to distinguish speech sounds while constructing meaning. The process of constructing meaning is listening comprehension. Speaking is a productive skill that requires the listener to use the meaning they have constructed to produce speech sounds to communicate a message. Speaking also requires attention to syntax, vocabulary, and pragmatics (the ability to use language in social situations). Oracy also refers to proficiency in oral expression. In an increasingly global society, collaboration skills are essential to the 21st century workforce, and successful collaboration relies heavily on communication, or oracy.

Research conducted by the National Panel for Language Minority Children and Youth (Cárdenas-Hagan, 2020) emphasizes that oral language proficiency should be a focus when students are learning English. Oral language skills should be developed organically and explicitly. Organic oral language development most often takes place through purposeful conversations in which parents and educators read and talk about books, ask questions, and use sophisticated vocabulary. Syntax, vocabulary, pragmatics, and discourse are components of oracy that can be developed organically, whereas phonological and morphological skills require explicit instruction.

Phonological awareness means that students can identify and mentally manipulate sounds, syllables, and words. These oral tasks don't involve print and include rhyming, alliteration, blending, and segmenting (Moats, 2020). Students also benefit when syntax and vocabulary are taught explicitly, although a balance of organic and purposeful conversation supports these skills as well. For example, through repeated conversations, students learn that the proper word order in English is *the big red crayon* rather than *the red big crayon*. Multilingual students need oral language development opportunities that are both organic and explicit to acquire English language and literacy.

Literacy

Literacy focuses on the language domains of *reading and writing*. Reading is a receptive language skill that involves decoding sounds and constructing meaning from written words (Kongsvik, n.d.). Scarborough's Reading Rope (The Reading League, 2022) is one framework that helps us understand how the brain learns to read; it consists of two main strands: language comprehension and word recognition. This rope is a visual metaphor for the development of skills over time that lead to skilled reading.

The language comprehension strand of the rope comprises many of the skills mentioned in our oracy section. Bilingual dyslexia therapist and speech pathologist Elsa Cárdenas-Hagan (2020) writes, "Oral language is also a basic skill that is necessary for a higher form of language, which includes reading and writing. Notably a student must have strong oral language skills in order to achieve high levels of literacy skills" (p. 16). Understanding how oral language supports reading and writing helps educators make informed decisions that support the language and literacy development of multilingual learners.

More specifically, it's important for educators to facilitate cross-linguistic connections for multilingual students. To do so, teachers don't need to be bilingual or multilingual. However, it's helpful to know the basics about languages. For example, understanding the unique facets of English can help teachers support students' linguistic connections. English is an alphabetic language with a deep orthography—that is, it uses symbols or combinations of symbols to represent its 44 speech sounds, which are strung together to make words. This is in contrast to a logographic language, such as Chinese, or to the syllabaries (written characters representing syllables) in the Cherokee and Japanese languages. In languages that are not alphabetic, characters or symbols represent syllables or word parts (morphemes) rather than a single sound (phoneme).

Orthography refers to the writing and spelling system of a language. English has multiple sounds for letters, making its orthography deep. In addition, English spellings can represent both phonemes and morphemes, both sound and meaning (Moats, 2020). We see this in words like *subway, subtopic,* and s*ubmarine,* where prefixes and suffixes clue us into the meaning of the word. English also borrows words from many other languages, meaning that a knowledge of word origins helps out in spelling. If you've ever watched a spelling bee, you know that one strategy to correctly spell words is to know the origin of the word (Moats, 2020). Being aware of fundamental information about the English language as compared to other languages helps build knowledge and empathy. What we're asking multilingual learners to do isn't easy.

Writing is a productive skill, similar to speaking, but it's much more complex. As author Joan Sedita (2023) states, "Proficient writers must integrate multiple skills, strategies, and techniques" (p. 13). Her writing rope graphic breaks down the skills needed for writing in the same way that Scarborough's Rope does for reading. Sedita's rope includes five components: critical thinking, syntax, text structure, writing craft, and transcription. In her book *The Writing Rope,* she notes that to be a proficient writer, working memory and executive functions—such as attention, goal setting, and self-regulation—are crucial. Writing requires proficiency in listening, speaking, and reading. This is why in language acquisition spaces, it's often said that writing is the last domain in which students reach proficiency. So many skills must be in place before students are ready to express themselves in written form.

Supporting oral language development is the most foundational method to develop writing skills in multilingual learners. Also, providing explicit instruction in writing strategies, specifically in the area of syntax, is essential. In my work with multilingual students, I have seen the most gains when focusing on developing students' syntactic awareness, or sentence sense. Direct explicit instruction on sentence structure, combined with activities such as sentence scrambles and elaboration, support syntactic awareness. As Sedita (2023) notes, "When students use their syntactic awareness to write sentences, they apply their knowledge of oral language to written language" (p. 60). Syntactic awareness is to writing what oral language is to reading. All students must develop these foundational skills to become literate, but multilingual students require targeted, direct, and explicit instruction to do so.

Although decoding phonemes is foundational to reading and understanding subject-verb agreement is foundational to writing, neither of these skills is the end goal. The purpose of being literate is to acquire and share information. The purpose is to learn. Once students learn to read, they must then make the key shift into reading to learn. Once students learn the basics of writing, they must make the key shift into writing to demonstrate understanding and share ideas. This is where background knowledge, vocabulary, and literacy knowledge become more prominent. We'll now focus on how engagement supports these three components.

Engagement

Over the years, many researchers have directly correlated engagement to academic achievement. When learners are actively engaged in learning tasks, they're more likely to remember and apply the concepts in the long term. Educational researcher Robert Marzano (2019) reminds us that engagement strategies "are not merely activities to be checked off; they are methods of creating a practice that combines your art with the science of noticing and reacting when students are not engaged" (p. 175).

The idea of teaching as an art and science has always resonated with me. It balances the neuroscience of learning with the creativity of crafting learning experiences. Student engagement is crafted by the conditions we create and the opportunities we offer students to take action as independent learners (Porosoff, 2023). I define student engagement as *visible interest and investment in a learning task, characterized by mental perseverance and concept attainment*. Of course, our classrooms are filled with students of varying abilities and interests, so it's unreasonable to expect that every lesson or learning task will engage every student every time. However, if we keep the unique interests of our students in mind, we're more likely to create environments that compel students to engage.

The foundation we laid with the building blocks of relationships, relevance, and rigor manifests in engagement. If we've been affirming and acknowledging our students' cultures and empowering them as learners while holding high expectations, then half the work of engagement is complete. The other half comes into play when we collaboratively plan, monitor engagement levels, adjust, and reengage students accordingly.

Porosoff (2023) also reflects that authentic engagement is a choice: "Authenticity means sharing our experiences, identities, histories, and ideas" (p. 3). And that choice involves risk. When students raise their hands to share information, they don't just risk being wrong; they risk being wrong in front of their peers, which may be why disengaged students don't raise their hands to share. Moreover, when students are disengaged, distracting behavior increases, thus the link between engagement and effective classroom management.

The foundation of classroom management is relationships. A lack of relational capital between teachers and students decreases the likelihood that lessons and learning tasks will feel relevant to students. In the absence of relational capital and in the absence of relevance, we can't begin to provide the rigor needed to call students up toward independent learning. If lessons and learning tasks are engaging, students are more eager to persevere toward concept attainment.

A significant component of engagement involves student talk. Reading and writing "float on a sea of talk" (Sedita, 2024). In fact, *learning* floats on a sea of talk. Working with a peer to edit an essay, collaborating on science labs, sharing problem-solving strategies, or debating historical events all require conversation, an ability that is a crucial component of being literate.

Authors Seidlitz and Perryman (2022) sum it up in their book *The 7 Steps to a Language-Rich Interactive Classroom*: "Literacy is more than just reading words on a page. It also includes the ability to engage students in meaningful conversations"

(p. 9). Structured conversations—such as turn-and-talk; Question, Signal, Stem, Share, Assess (QSSSA); and think-pair-share—provide ways for students to engage in meaningful conversations. Appendix C, Instructional Routines for Structured Conversations, provides a chart with several conversation strategies that leverage student talk to boost engagement.

I've often heard the comment "The one doing the talking is doing the learning." But before students can discuss what they're learning, they must actively listen to what people are saying about the topic, consider the topic, process what they've heard, then construct their own thoughts about the topic. So much brain power is required before words are even uttered! Using brain power to share learning and respond to others' ideas increases both engagement and concept retention.

Layer 3. Linguistically Accommodated Instruction

The third and final layer to quality language acquisition instruction refers to linguistic accommodations. This layer strikes at the heart of the needs of multilingual learners. To access universal Tier 1 instruction, multilingual learners require instruction infused with language scaffolds that enable them to learn content and acquire English simultaneously. When linguistic scaffolds are not provided, multilingual learners cannot access the content. This lack of access slows both the student's acquisition of English and their ability to learn content, thus widening gaps. It's not the achievement gap that widens but the *access* gap.

Let's begin by clarifying definitions. Generally speaking, teachers implement academic accommodations to reduce barriers and provide students with learning differences equal access to learning. *Academic* accommodations don't change the content students learn. Instead, they adjust how content is taught, accessed, or assessed. *Linguistic* accommodations decrease the barrier that language differences create. These adjustments or scaffolds can apply to pacing, materials, or instruction.

I think of linguistic accommodations as scaffolds that are documented, making them legal requirements that multilingual learners are entitled to receive. The U.S. Supreme Court case *Lau v. Nichols* (1974) affirmed the rights of multilingual students to meaningfully participate in educational programs, noting that the students who did not speak English were "certain to find their classroom experiences wholly incomprehensible." In addition, the Department of Justice in conjunction with the Department of Education released a "Dear Colleague" letter in 2015 reminding states, districts, and schools of their obligations under federal law to ensure that English language learners have equal access to a high-quality education and the opportunity to achieve their full academic potential.

Linguistic accommodations can be grouped into two types: material/resource or instructional. Material scaffolds are tangible scaffolds teachers provide to students, such as sentence stems or word banks. Instructional scaffolds are actions that teachers perform during the lesson delivery or lesson cycle, such as organizing reading into chunks or using think-alouds. (Access to linguistic glossaries by proficiency are shared at the end of this chapter in the "Make Your Moves" section, and visit www.coachreflective.org/free-downloads for more resources.) Providing linguistically accommodated instruction that is comprehensible, differentiated, and scaffolded helps close the access gap.

Comprehensible

When faced with teaching multilingual students, teachers are often concerned about the obstacles presented by the communication barrier. The most effective way to deal with this is by providing teachers with low-lift strategies that make communication comprehensible for multilingual learners.

The idea of comprehensible input has been popularized by linguist and educational researcher Stephen Krashen (1982). His theory of second language acquisition suggests that to acquire the language, students need comprehensible input and low-stress opportunities for output. His hypothesis about affective filters—those walls that go up between us and our learning—are important to note as we unpack low-stress opportunities for output. Krashen points out that affective variables can raise the affective filter and form a mental block that prevents language acquisition. Anytime we ask multilingual learners to share their thinking aloud or in writing, we can ensure tasks are low stress by lowering students' affective filter with language scaffolds that support their ability to produce output. Figure 2.3 illustrates the variables that can affect a student's affective filter.

Imagine you're in a professional learning session at a conference and the presenter suddenly points to you and asks you to share your thoughts. Are you elated or stressed to share in this room full of strangers? It may depend on a number of variables: Are you confident in the topic at hand? Are you an introvert or an extrovert? Does speaking in front of large groups make you anxious? Consider that this scenario involves an adult and a professional educator sharing their thinking aloud in front of peers *in their native language* on a topic in which they have background knowledge. Our multilingual students have to face this same challenge, but they're working in an unfamiliar language on a topic they may still be learning. It's necessary to put structures in place that make the classroom safe for multilingual students to take risks with a new language—but it's also kind.

FIGURE 2.3

What Is the Affective Filter?

A metaphor that describes an invisible psychological filter or wall that can arise, based on student variables; when this wall goes up, it can hinder the student from engaging in classroom instruction and acquiring a second language.

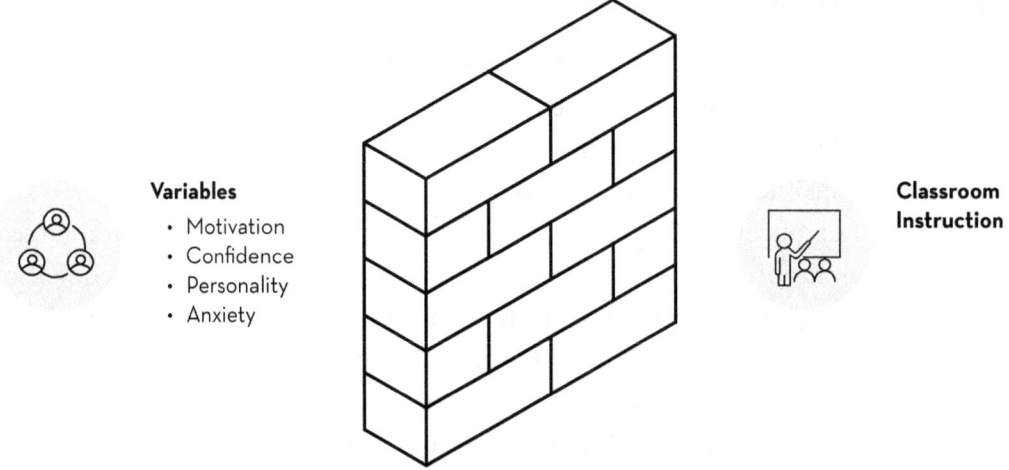

Variables
- Motivation
- Confidence
- Personality
- Anxiety

Classroom Instruction

Let's imagine a 3rd grade teacher posing the following question during a science lesson: *What might happen in an ecosystem if one organism from the food chain is removed?* How would you coach this teacher in making the content more comprehensible? What linguistic and material scaffolds might support multilingual students in sharing their responses? What instructional scaffold could a teacher use to support students' oral responses? Figure 2.4 suggests some teacher dialogue and actions to implement those accommodations.

What aligns to your thinking? What would you suggest to teachers you support? What would you change?

FIGURE 2.4

Linguistic Accommodations: Teacher Dialogue and Actions

Teacher Dialogue	Teacher Actions
"What might happen to an ecosystem if one organism is removed from the food chain?"	Teacher points to a graphic of a food chain that has an X over one animal.
"Think for a moment about what might happen if the grasshopper goes missing."	Teacher places their hand on their chin and models a "thinking face."
"If the grasshopper is missing from the food chain, then...."	Teacher points to a sentence stem and reads it.
"Let's say this sentence stem together."	Teacher tracks the print while rereading the sentence stem slowly.
"Turn to your partner and share your ideas using the sentence stem. Partner A will go first, followed by partner B. I will know you and your partner are finished talking when you high-five each other and then turn and face the board."	Teacher circulates among students as they talk, listening in to check for understanding. After the conversations end, teacher calls on a multilingual student to share their response using the sentence stem.

The accommodations listed in Figure 2.4 lower students' affective filters, providing an entry point for students to take in content (input) and show what they know (output). Another way to make it safe for students to share their thinking on a topic is through conversations on nonacademic topics. Starting the year off with structured conversations that include "get to know you" questions will contribute to a safe and engaging environment. It also provides an opportunity for students to get to know one another. Figure 2.5 illustrates steps you can take to make instruction comprehensible and overcome the affective filter.

Once the teacher has cultivated a safe environment for students, they can select, plan, and embed linguistic accommodations into the lesson delivery. This brings us to the next component of linguistically accommodated instruction—it's differentiated.

FIGURE 2.5

Making Instruction Comprehensible

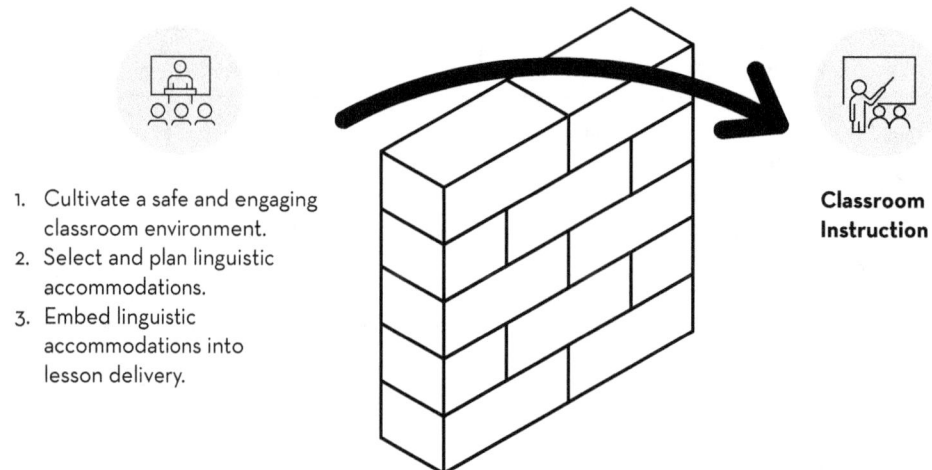

1. Cultivate a safe and engaging classroom environment.
2. Select and plan linguistic accommodations.
3. Embed linguistic accommodations into lesson delivery.

Classroom Instruction

Differentiated

Differentiation refers to tailoring the content, process, products, or learning environment to meet individual student needs (Tomlinson, n.d.). The key phrase here is "individual student needs." We need to base our linguistic accommodations on the language proficiency of the student. A student who is at the beginning level of language proficiency will need many more linguistic accommodations than a student who is nearly English proficient. We must remember that students receiving linguistic support services have an end goal, which is to reclassify them as English proficient, based on the criteria set forth by each U.S. state.

In light of this, it's important to be strategic in the linguistic accommodations we select so we're simultaneously supporting and challenging multilingual learners (Snyder & Fenner, 2021). One of the greatest "aha" moments I had was when I began coaching teachers on how to select linguistic accommodations based on students' proficiency levels. Figure 2.6 places scaffolds in categories based on language proficiency ranges. When planning lessons, it's best to begin by putting scaffolds in place for students to receive comprehensible input (listening and reading) and follow that with putting scaffolds in place to support low-stress output (speaking and writing). That's why the receptive domains of listening and reading are listed first, followed by the expressive domains of speaking and writing.

FIGURE 2.6

Proficiency Levels and Descriptors

Newcomer	Emergent	Early Intermediate	Intermediate	Near Proficient
Silent Period or Sounds	**Words**	**Phrases**	**Sentences**	**Discourse**
• Visuals and graphics • Realia • Rephrase, repeat, slow down • Gestures for emphasis • Bilingual dictionary or glossary • Peer or native language support • Translation of texts, words, and phrases • Nonparticipation in conversations • Wait time • Response signals • Drawing and pictorial representations	• Visuals and graphics • Realia • Rephrase, repeat, slow down • Gestures for emphasis • Clarification of words and phrases • Bilingual dictionary or glossary • Peer or native language support • Translation of texts, words, and phrases • Wait time • Response signals • Drawing and pictorial representations • Sentence frames/stems • Modeling pronunciation	• Rephrase, repeat, slow down • Recasting responses • Clarification of words and phrases • Adapted text • Wait time • Response signals • Sentence frames/stems • Modeling pronunciation • Providing oral phrases and sentence stems • Paragraph frames • Word banks • Preteaching vocabulary • Activating and building background knowledge	• Recasting responses • Paragraph frames • Organizing reading into chunks • Modeling and thinking aloud • Extra time to complete assignments • Scaffolded writing assignments	• Modeling and thinking aloud • Extra time to complete assignments • Scaffolded writing assignments

The accommodations we select and embed must match not only the student's proficiency level but also their strengths and needs. We should form a hypothesis as we plan lessons, test our hypothesis as we deliver the lesson, and then get creative as we notice the student's response. Much like a stand-up comedian at improv, teachers continually take in data from their students that enable them to monitor and adjust on the spot. Teaching *is* both art and science. The science is in the planning, the art happens spontaneously as we teach—and the magic occurs when we balance the two.

Targeted

In the context of providing linguistically accommodated instruction, *targeted* means providing temporary support to facilitate students toward independently completing tasks once they've acquired and become proficient in English (Snyder & Fenner, 2021). Our objective is to grow not only students' language proficiency but also their ability to learn independently. When we target scaffolds to meet the precise linguistic needs of students, it supports them in their zone of proximal development, that precious space between what a learner can do independently and what they can do with support. We use linguistic scaffolds to bridge the space, moving more and more tasks toward the student's zone of actual development, where they can complete academic tasks independently.

A key shift in my practice with multilingual students, particularly newcomers, was teaching them to advocate for themselves. Providing students with sentence stems and the language they might use to request specific scaffolds empowered them, fostering ownership of their learning. This strengthens students' self-efficacy. According to Hammond (2014), "Students' efficacy beliefs are positively associated with how long they will persevere at a learning task" (p. 114). Such beliefs also set the stage for students to develop an academic mindset affirming that "ability and competence grow with [their] effort" (p. 114).

If developing independent learners who are English proficient is our end goal, then the temporary nature of scaffolds is important to keep in mind as we plan instruction. We know we're hitting our goal when we're able to remove scaffolds intended for lower levels of language proficiency and replace them with ones suitable for students at higher levels of language proficiency. Students at the newcomer and emerging levels acquire language rapidly. Teachers should be monitoring and adjusting accommodations at a steady pace. However, around the intermediate to near-proficient stages, language growth happens at a slower pace. It's vital at this point to embed scaffolds that target the specific strengths and needs of the individual student.

We can now tie all these layers of quality language acquisition instruction together in an overarching cycle that grows language proficiency.

A Four-Step Process

We began with the first layer—asset-based and equity-driven practices—by *identifying* the affective, instructional, and linguistic needs of our students. Teachers do this work with all students at the start of the school year. When working with multilingual students, it's important to note their assets, funds of knowledge, language proficiency levels, and general learning behaviors. Second, we *select scaffolds* that align with students' English language proficiency levels. Once we document these scaffolds, they become linguistic accommodations that multilingual learners are legally entitled to receive. Then comes the mental and scientific work of embedding these accommodations into our lesson plans to ensure we're providing comprehensible input and opportunities for low-stress output.

Our third step is the artistry, the heart of our work—*instruction*. Here we create literacy-rich environments infused with linguistic accommodations that simultaneously support and challenge our students. Finally, in our fourth and last step, we *monitor* student progress through informal and formal assessments that often lead us to identify new assets and learning behaviors. Then the cycle begins again.

This four-step process is captured in Figure 2.7. The steps are sequential, but they also repeat in cycles of continuous improvement that grow students' language proficiency. As we engage in the coaching models described in later chapters, we'll see these steps in action.

Tying It Up

In this chapter, we've explored the conditions that ensure that multilingual learners acquire English. We began with the mindset and motivation behind quality language acquisition instruction by unpacking asset-based mindsets and equity-driven practices. This laid the foundation to explore the moves that support quality language acquisition instruction, language- and literacy-rich environments, and linguistic accommodations. After unpacking these layers, we then considered how we might sequence them to grow the language proficiency of multilingual students. Engaging in the behaviors associated with each layer in a cyclical manner ensures we continually improve our educational practices and the educational opportunities of multilingual learners.

FIGURE 2.7

Growing Language Proficiency

1 Learn	2 Plan	3 Teach	4 Reflect
Who is the student as a learner?	**What scaffolds does the student need to develop language proficiency?**	**How does the lesson design intentionally support language development?**	**How did the learner respond?**
• Assets • Funds of knowledge • Language proficiency • Learning style and needs	• Proficiency-based • Instructional • Linguistic • Material	• Language rich • Literacy rich • Comprehensible • Differentiated • Scaffolded	• Progress monitoring • Qualitative and quantitative data • Formative and summative data • District and campus-based data

Mind Your Ms

Maximize Your Motivation

Review Figure 2.2—The Asset-Based Mindset Versus the Deficit-Based Mindset—and consider journaling your responses to the following questions:

- When thinking of relationships, relevance, and rigor, which do you believe is most important? Why?
- What asset-based characteristics are you committed to growing toward? Why?
- How will you know you're growing in this area? What are your success criteria?
- Have you noticed any deficit-based characteristics in your context?

Mold Your Mindset

Research and read about instructional practices for culturally and linguistically diverse students. Here are some suggestions:

- *Culturally Responsive Teaching and the Brain* (2014), by Zaretta Hammond
- *Culturally Responsive Teaching for Multilingual Learners: Tools for Equity* (2021), by Sydney Snyder and Diane Staehr Fenner
- *Unlocking English Learners' Potential: Strategies for Making Content Accessible* (2017), by Diane Staehr Fenner and Sydney Snyder
- *The New Art and Science of Teaching (More Than Fifty New Instructional Strategies for Academic Success)* (2017), by Robert J. Marzano

Make Your Moves

Visit the linguistic accommodation glossary found at www.coachreflective.org/free-downloads and choose a proficiency level to review.

- Place a star beside the accommodations that are most natural for you to implement.
- Highlight the accommodations you want to learn more about.
- Review the layers of quality language acquisition instruction.
- Identify what actions you take that support each layer.
- Based on those actions, rank to what degree each layer is currently represented in your work.

3

Coaching Moves

"So, what exactly *is* your role?" This question came up regularly in my first few months of coaching. My large suburban school district had made the decision to pivot away from the ESL teacher role at the elementary level, replacing it with a language coach role. I was in the inaugural class of language coaches, or LCs as we were called. Each campus had instructional coaches who worked with teachers to build their capacity and ensure curriculum implementation, as well as digital learning coaches, or DLCs, who worked with teachers to integrate technology into instruction.

These coaching roles were established and understood, but where did my new role fit in? This was the question principals and coaches alike wondered. We all knew that language coaches would be a part of the school instructional leadership team, but for the purpose of doing what exactly? We also knew that language coaches were to move away from pulling out small groups of students to work with (unless they were at the beginning levels of language proficiency) and, instead, were to focus on coaching teachers—but what did that look like daily? How would this benefit students and teachers? And would this change make a difference?

The Need for a New Model

According to the National Clearinghouse for English Language Acquisition (NCELA, n.d.), the number of English learners increased nationwide by 2.3 percent between the 2000–2001 and 2019–2020 school years, by almost a million and a half more students. My home state of Texas has seen an increase of 80 percent, which translates into roughly half a million students. Texas leads with 19.6 percent of its student population characterized as English learners, followed by California at 18.6 percent and New Mexico at 16.5 percent (NCELA, n.d.). The National Center for Education Statistics (NCES, 2024) similarly reports an increase of 5.1 million English learners between 2010 and 2019. In my district, these statistics prompted systemic change. A steady increase in multilingual students enrolling and qualifying for linguistic support, coupled with stagnant language proficiency scores on the state assessment for multilingual learners, further supported the need for a new approach.

Our aim has been to shift from an exclusive to an inclusive model. An exclusive model designates one staff member to serve as the point person for multilingual students. This instructional leader often goes it alone, typically becoming the sole linguistic expert—and the sole keeper of that expertise. In contrast, an inclusive model engages all stakeholders, from the content teacher to the principal. The coach shares their own passion for advocacy and linguistic expertise while building the capacity of the school community to serve multilingual students. In the years following the launch and development of our language coaching program, we have experienced tremendous mental shifts and measurable improvements. We're now far more likely to hear instructional leaders identify issues to address, make suggestions, and champion the needs of multilingual students.

Sharing the "why" is vital, but the knowledge that leads to a change in praxis is all about the "how." What coaching moves help teachers and leaders best meet the needs of their multilingual students? How can coaching build the capacity of the school community to better serve these students? When partnering with teachers to advocate for multilingual learners, it's essential to have a system of strategies that can both anchor and guide our work.

In my first year as a coach, I attended multiple training sessions, each one rooted in a slightly different theory with a slightly different focus. Our program was new, and I was floating in a sea of coaching practices, trying to apply each new piece of learning, then waiting to see the results. At a district meeting set aside specifically for language coaches, my mentor Laurea Myers introduced a coaching continuum; it showed the behaviors a language coach could engage in listed on a continuum from surface level to deep. Over the years as I've applied it to my work, it's evolved into the chart depicted in Figure 3.1. This framework focuses on three levels of language coaching: consultative, reflective, and collaborative. We'll now look at each of these levels in depth.

FIGURE 3.1

Levels of Language Coaching

Consultative	Reflective	Collaborative
Consultative coaching is focused on building relationships. It's performed on an as-needed basis and often targets a specific inquiry or issue.	Reflective coaching creates a space for the coach and coachee to think together. This level of coaching requires intentional partnering for the purpose of enhancing instruction and student success.	Collaborative coaching is the most intense level of coaching, requiring full partnership. The focus is on developing practitioner expertise through a cycle of deliberate practice that leads to student success.
• Advocate for multilingual language learners • Engage in committed listening • Build and maintain trust • Witness the good • Provide resources • Share information	• Paraphrase • Offer reflective questioning • Provide feedback • Model lessons • Monitor student progress • Review student work/artifacts • Co-plan • Set student goals	• Engage in all actions at the reflective level • Set practitioner goals • Self-rate implementation • Journal • Rehearse • Review film or audio

Level 1. Consultative Coaching

Consultative coaching is usually the first step in coaching. It focuses on building relationships—because coaching is partnership. Adults learn best when they feel connected to others because we're wired for connection. John Gottman, relationship psychologist, and his coauthor Joan DeClaire use the term *bids for connection* to describe the small behaviors we engage in when we want to connect (Knight, 2015). A bid can be a smile, a question, a conversation starter, or a random act of kindness. They're all building blocks toward rapport.

Many behaviors that the coach engages in at the consultative level are ongoing. Committed listening, witnessing the good, and providing resources will be something you do all year long. Other behaviors, such as advocating for students, maintaining rapport, and sharing information, may evolve over time. Although the consultative level is where we start with all teachers, it's often appropriate for addressing a specific inquiry. For example, after grading several assignments, a teacher may notice that a student consistently makes second language errors or that their multilingual students are not progressing at the same rate as their monolingual ones. Or a teacher may receive a new student at the beginning levels of language proficiency and reach out to the coach for support. To meet the needs of both teachers and students, it's important to know what strategies work best. Let's unpack each of them.

Advocating for Multilingual Learners

This strategy is both a mindset and an action. When we meet with a teacher or team, our primary objective is to advocate for linguistic strategies and instructional practices that will best meet the needs of multilingual learners. Many times, this means navigating between student needs and teacher preferences.

It also requires courage. In our advocacy, we must not sacrifice what's best for students to make adults comfortable. We must be strategic as we share information; this means connecting the strategies we suggest to existing instructional practices, making them low lift but high yield. For example, a teacher repeating a sentence stem is a quick and easy thing to do to encourage students to speak in complete sentences. The coach needs to gracefully meet teachers where they are, while, at the same time, resolutely spurring them forward.

Engaging in Committed Listening

Kathy Kee and the Results Coaching group (2010) describe committed listening this way: "When we listen with commitment, we convey, 'I care about what you have to say, and I'm listening with all my senses so that I fully understand an issue from your perspective'" (p. 95). Listening is the foundation of any healthy human relationship. Without committed listening, we can't be sure how to best advocate for multilingual learners or which resources to provide, and we certainly can't build trust or maintain rapport.

Committed listening is a foundational communication move because it honors the teacher's voice. In a post-pandemic world in which teachers have exited the profession en masse, having a coach or leader who truly listens is vital. When we listen with commitment, we set aside judgment and advice to be fully present; we pause to allow the teacher's words to sink in, then we paraphrase and ask clarifying questions. This can give you a clear picture of how well you're able to honor teachers' voices.

Building and Maintaining Trust

This is where we build connections using those bids we mentioned. It's seeing a need and filling a need. It's keeping an eye on the class while the 5th grade teacher runs to the lounge to grab a cupcake. It's being an extra pair of hands during kindergarten lunch period the first few weeks of school. Of course, we mustn't fall into the trap of doing too many clerical tasks or being seen as an errand runner, a risk that new coaches need to be mindful of. Nevertheless, in these small acts of service we demonstrate servant leadership, and we communicate what we all want to hear as human beings: "I see you."

Thought leader Brené Brown (2018) breaks down trust using the BRAVING acronym: Boundaries, Reliability, Accountability, Vault, Integrity, Nonjudgment, and Grace. Each word highlights an essential element of building trust. Most notably for coaching are integrity and grace. We reveal our integrity when we communicate that employing linguistic scaffolds for multilingual learners isn't just "one more thing to do" but rather an essential part of providing Tier 1 instruction. Presuming positive intent enables us to respond graciously when a teacher laments that they "have to have another newcomer in their class." It enables us to look past the deficit-based mindset to view the teacher's anxiety about providing quality instruction to a student who doesn't speak English, yet.

Once we've built a trusting relationship with teachers, our focus is on maintaining rapport through reliability—that is, we do what we say we'll do. If we say we'll provide a resource, we do so. If we commit to a co-teaching cycle, we go through each of its components. We must be careful not to underdeliver—or overpromise. This is where boundaries come into play. We can violate our boundaries or exceed our own capacities in an attempt to meet unrealistic commitments we've made. At worst, we may need to backtrack on a commitment, eroding reliability and fracturing trust. To maintain rapport, we must maintain a healthy balance with each element of trust.

Witnessing the Good

When we witness the good, we're on the lookout for all the great instructional practices taking place around us. We train our brains to notice and name the positive things we observe. Instead of saying, "I can tell your multilingual students feel successful in your classroom," you might say, "I can tell you've made your multilingual students feel successful by giving them sentence stems and word banks during structured conversations." This type of comment doesn't just notice the effect; it also names the exact moves that caused that effect. We can witness the good with a note or a shout-out in a school newsletter or simply by telling the person. These are good ways to communicate that we see people.

Providing Resources

Finding ways to save teachers time is a great superpower to have and develop as a coach. Providing resources enables us to meet student needs as we support instruction and build trust. At team collaborative planning meetings, we listen to find ways to support instruction linguistically. We can offer templates for a structured conversation strategy, a background-building anticipation guide, or a soft or hard copy of a vocabulary activity.

Sharing Information

We do this so regularly that we barely notice it. Providing information can be a great way to deepen pedagogy and improve instruction—if we add more intentionality behind it. For example, at the beginning of a school year, the language coach is responsible for ensuring that teachers can access their students' linguistic profiles, including the students' latest language assessment scores and any linguistic accommodations teachers used with them the previous school year. After my first year as a language coach, instead of sending teachers an email that detailed how they could access this information, I made folders that included a printed copy of their students' linguistic accommodations and language assessment scores. I also included a one-pager that detailed how serving their multilingual students would look throughout the year, and I listed proficiency level descriptors we would use to monitor linguistic growth. I simply made the required information more accessible and comprehensible. The key to effectively sharing information is ensuring that the target audience can easily access and apply that information.

Level 2. Reflective Coaching

In the first year of coaching, it's wise to focus your practice on mastering the moves at the consultative level while you learn your new role. Even as an experienced coach, you'll find that you may remain in consultative coaching with certain teachers or teams, based on their needs and dynamics.

Reflective coaching ups the game; it's about creating a space where two educators can think together with the express purpose of enhancing instruction and achieving measurable improvements in student success rates. Reaching a place where a teacher feels safe and comfortable to be open and think aloud requires trust built over time using many of the strategies we use at the consultative level. At the reflective level of coaching, we're preparing to directly serve the students in the teacher's classroom.

Perhaps you've spent time collaboratively planning with a team of teachers and one teacher wants you to model a structured conversation or observe a lesson and provide feedback. Maybe you've provided a vocabulary resource and now a teacher would like you to look at the work samples of their multilingual students. It's important to note that these levels are also a continuum, so we'll flow back and forth along the levels, and we won't be engaging in every strategy listed under every level. Here are some strategies that are appropriate at this level of coaching.

Paraphrasing

Kathy Kee and colleagues (2010) unpack paraphrasing this way: "Paraphrasing is intended to align the people in a conversation and create a safe environment for thinking" (p. 107). What does it take to create a safe environment for thinking? Feeling heard and valued are two prerequisites that come to mind. If I know I'm being listened to, I'm more likely to engage in a conversation because I don't risk being rejected or casting my proverbial pearls before swine. I feel valued, as though what I have to say makes a difference to the listener.

Coaches can provide safety through paraphrasing. We communicate that we've heard our thinking partner and that we value their thoughts. Paraphrasing also makes thinking come alive; when I hear my words repeated in a slightly different manner, I hear my own thoughts aloud. Further, a coach can recast a comment by adding value statements. For example, if a teacher says, "My class can't handle turn-and-talk; they get too off topic during class discussions," a coach can paraphrase with a value statement: "That makes sense; you want the learning time to be valuable and structured for student learning." Paraphrasing enables us to begin the process of thinking together because we're on the same page.

Engaging in Reflective Questioning

Reflective questioning enables us to use an open-ended, nonjudgmental question to draw out the thinking of our conversation partner (Knight, 2015). More often than not, the teacher has the answer; they just need the gift of time to process aloud to reach that answer. A question that presumes positive intent can be a great catalyst to enhancing instruction. Let's go back to that teacher's comment about disliking the strategy of turn-and-talk. Asking, "How could we use sentence stems or a randomizing tool to encourage students to stay on topic?" would be a helpful follow-up question. Such questions are designed to get teachers and coaches thinking aloud together.

Providing Feedback

According to the researchers at Visible Learning (Corwin Visible Learning Plus, n.d.), feedback in the classroom is "information allowing a learner to reduce the gap between what is evident currently and what could or should be the case." When a language coach provides feedback to a teacher on how to implement linguistic strategies, it can open up space for the coach and teacher to think together about how to best instruct multilingual students. The key to feedback is in the delivery. It's not advice, praise, or evaluation; it's information about how we're doing in our efforts to reach a goal (Wiggins, 2021). The phrase that resonates most with me is "our efforts to reach a goal" because it clarifies that feedback is most valuable when we have a specific goal in mind. The goal can be based on what the teacher hopes to achieve or on a set of linguistic strategies designated by your school district or campus.

Feedback most often takes place during coaching conversations when the teacher and coach are reflecting on a coaching minicycle or on a co-taught lesson during a co-teaching cycle. But it can also take place when we observe students during a lesson. Teachers naturally request feedback: "How do you think that went? Should I do something differently?" In these situations, it's best to provide *appreciation* feedback, then offer to come back if they would like coaching feedback.

When we go into classrooms to observe students, this should truly be our focus. We will undoubtedly notice moves the teacher uses that enhance or detract from learning. It's important to *keep our focus on the student*, especially if that's the reason we gave for being welcomed into the classroom in the first place. In situations where we're tasked to provide unsolicited feedback, perhaps as a part of learning walks with school leadership, we'll want to clarify which linguistic strategies we're going to look at. Are the teachers clear on which strategies we're going to observe? Have they had professional learning experiences to explore these strategies? We need to be able to answer "yes" to these questions before offering feedback. Otherwise, we run the risk of eroding trust by coming in to monitor expectations we never made clear. We'll explore what feedback in minicycles and co-teaching look like in later chapters.

Modeling Lessons

Modeling lessons is an excellent way to build teacher capacity and create an opportunity for thinking together. When a new linguistic or instructional strategy is introduced to staff, offer to model it in a teacher's classroom. This has layered benefits. First, it enables the teacher to witness the strategy in real time with their students; it's a visual that can spark further ideas. In addition, nothing communicates competence to teachers like being able to walk in their shoes. Teachers often wonder if coaches and administrators still know what it's like to actually teach a classroom of students. Modeling lessons in classrooms keeps coaches and administrators grounded in that reality. And competence breeds confidence. If a teacher sees a coach competently working with their students, their confidence in that coach's ability increases. Thus, modeling a lesson is both a trust-building and a capacity-building opportunity.

It's wise to structure the modeled lesson so there are opportunities to debrief before and afterward. Before the lesson, you could ask any questions regarding the classroom environment that might make the model successful. You can also provide the teacher with look-fors and ask them to observe and evaluate *your* lesson. Model vulnerability. Afterward, you can unpack their observations and discuss what they noticed and wondered about and how they could see using the strategy moving forward.

Monitoring Student Progress

The Center on Multi-Tiered System of Supports (n.d.) defines *progress monitoring* as

> the ongoing, frequent collection and use of formal data in order to (1) assess students' performance, (2) quantify a student's rate of improvement or responsiveness to instruction or intervention, and (3) evaluate the effectiveness of instruction and intervention using valid and reliable measures.

In many cases, decisions regarding formal data collection are made for us by our states and school districts. This includes all the different types of assessments, from screenings and diagnostic assessments to specific progress-monitoring tools. For coaching purposes, we analyze the formal data collected and pair them with informal qualitative and quantitative data to make decisions about a student's educational needs. Informal data can include anecdotal notes, daily grades, and speaking assessments captured on video and audio recording platforms. Formative assessment is the most useful when coaching for multilingual learners because the teacher or instructional coach can collect the data before and during instruction with the intent of using them to change or modify instruction (Gibbons et al., 2018). In an era of high-stakes testing and intense accountability, instructional leaders and teachers can be data rich yet information poor. We can leverage reflective coaching to mitigate the onslaught of data created by the many assessments our students take.

Student progress monitoring as a reflective coaching move means creating a reflective space for teachers to consider the linguistic and academic needs and progress of multilingual learners by using reflective questions and paraphrasing and by reviewing student work and artifacts. We review student artifacts to monitor progress, and we monitor progress to determine if the linguistic scaffolds provided to students are effective. Have we seen an increase in language proficiency and concept attainment?

Progress monitoring and reviewing student artifacts are most likely to occur when implementing coaching models that are focused more particularly on student goals, such as in Inclusion with a Purpose and the Co-Teaching Cycle. Other opportunities might include data meetings following assessment windows or during meetings with a multi-tiered system of support team to plan and monitor Tier 2 and 3 programming for multilingual students. Whether you're working directly with a teacher or as a member of a team, the key to successful progress monitoring is asking reflective questions and providing resources and information. We want these conversations to be insightful and invigorating. Teachers should walk away with new perspectives and tools that move students closer toward English language proficiency.

For example, when reviewing a work sample from a science assignment, a teacher may notice that the students performed well on multiple-choice questions but struggled to respond to short-answer questions. Of her eight multilingual students, she sees that three didn't even attempt to answer the short-answer questions. She concludes that "writing is too hard for these three. I think they have a basic understanding of the standard, but writing is hard for multilingual learners." She's correct. You have often told your staff that writing is the last domain to fully develop among multilingual learners. However, instead of simply agreeing and giving in to these expectations, you could ask, "Would the opportunity to speak rather than write on this assignment help those students show mastery? What if we used a technology platform so they could record their responses orally?" The questions and the resource suggested enable you to look at alternate ways to address the quality of student work. They validate the teacher's concern while nudging them toward an action that can hold students accountable and push them toward oral language proficiency. Reviewing student work allows for the collaborative thinking that defines reflective coaching.

Co-Planning

Co-planning presents the ultimate opportunity for educators to "think together." Co-planning is most commonly done with grade- and department-level teaching teams as they plan weekly lessons and monthly units. (We devote an entire chapter—Chapter 5—to this coaching model.) It's also a component of our Co-Teaching Cycle, another coaching model we'll explore. However, co-planning as a coaching move refers to the more isolated moments of crafting a specific lesson delivery sequence with an individual teacher. This can occur when a teacher wants to target student engagement or academic vocabulary or embed a specific linguistic scaffold into their lesson delivery. Perhaps the teacher has sought you out, an administrator has suggested that the teacher collaborate with you, or you're simply interested in implementing a strategy you shared while delivering professional learning.

Although these scenarios are consultative in nature, they lend themselves to reflective coaching. These single co-planning sessions can develop into longer mini-cycles or co-teaching cycles. During these one-on-one co-planning sessions, a coach is grounded in the ideas of coaching for language proficiency (which we discussed in Chapter 2) and coaching through collaborative planning (which we'll focus on in Chapter 5). This ensures that content and lesson delivery is linguistically accommodated and language rich. It also ensures that our co-planning time truly creates a space to build teacher capacity where we can offer them the tools they need to succeed with their multilingual learners.

Setting Student Goals

"Goals challenge students," notes Bryan Goodwin and colleagues (2022) in *The New Classroom Instruction That Works*. "They also challenge teachers to be clear about what exactly they want students to learn and why" (p. 33). The authors unpack the importance of, as well as the process of, helping students commit to learning through setting, monitoring, and receiving feedback on goals. As a coaching move, goal setting can vary in its intensity and use. Goal setting with a teacher or a team may occur during a multi-tiered system of support meeting. Or a teacher might reach out informally to a coach before asking a team to collaborate with them on specific concerns they have about a student. In this case, rather than commit to a more time-intensive coaching model, it might be helpful to confer with the teacher—or with the teacher *and* student—to craft a linguistic goal.

The key to success in using goal setting as a coaching move is in the dialogue that takes place when we confer with the teacher and establish how we'll monitor success using feedback. This cultivates clarity on current student levels of performance, as well as on what specific skills we should target to move a student toward English language proficiency. During these conferring sessions, a coach is also leveraging key communication moves, such as reflective questioning and paraphrasing, to reach a common understanding of students' needs and craft a goal that meets those needs.

When crafting a goal, it's important to adhere to a goal-setting framework, such as SMART. Setting Specific, Measurable, Achievable, Relevant, and Timely goals for student progress will ensure results. The measurable part of the goal lends itself to establishing a set time to reconnect with the teacher formally or informally to evaluate success. Depending on the student's needs, you may wish to include the student in the process. If that's not feasible, it would be beneficial to share a goal you've crafted with the student. In Chapter 4, we focus on the student-centered coaching models of Goal Setting and Inclusion with a Purpose, where we'll look at specific goal-setting guidelines for multilingual students, as well as how to include students in the process.

Level 3. Collaborative Coaching

Collaborative coaching is the most intense level of language coaching because it requires full partnership. The focus is on building practitioner expertise, the practitioner being both the teacher and the coach. Although the coach may initiate many of the moves at this level, each move is highly collaborative and reciprocal, resulting in both shared power and shared learning (Knight, 2017). The moves at this level require vulnerability and a substantial time commitment. It takes vulnerability to self-rate your work and review and discuss a video or an audio recording of your teaching. It takes time to analyze and use data or engage in journaling. Although collaborative coaching is the most intense level, it's also where you, as the coach, will likely spend the least percentage of your overall coaching time because you're not coaching everyone in this way. In the meme'd words of Sweet Brown, a.k.a. Kimberly Wilkins, "Ain't nobody got time for that!"

Veteran coaches—those who have been in the same coaching role *and* on the same campus for a minimum of three years—might typically spend about 20 percent of their coaching time at the collaborative coaching level. Knowing how to manage the precious commodity of time is crucial. As a coach of coaches, I often find that those in coaching roles tend to hold themselves to unattainable time commitments. Coaches lead from the middle; they're neither the administrator who gives directives nor the teacher who works in the trenches. Rather, they're influencers. Coaches become adept at "lifting up" truths and ideas that they don't always have the power to implement or enforce. Leading from the middle requires self-awareness, effective communication, systems thinking, and resilience. It's complex work that requires strategy—and the ability to manage time. Figure 3.2 suggests some general time commitments coaches might make at each coaching level by years of experience.

Collaborative coaching is also intense because its aim is deliberate practice, which James Clear (2020) describes as purposeful and systematic. It requires focused attention on a specific goal, and it's set apart by feedback that measures progress and holds people accountable. Coaches enable teachers to measure their progress, to see what they can't see. "One consistent finding across disciplines," Clear writes, "is that coaches are often essential for sustaining deliberate practice. In many cases, it is nearly impossible to both perform a task and measure your progress at the same time."

FIGURE 3.2

Coaching Level Time Commitments

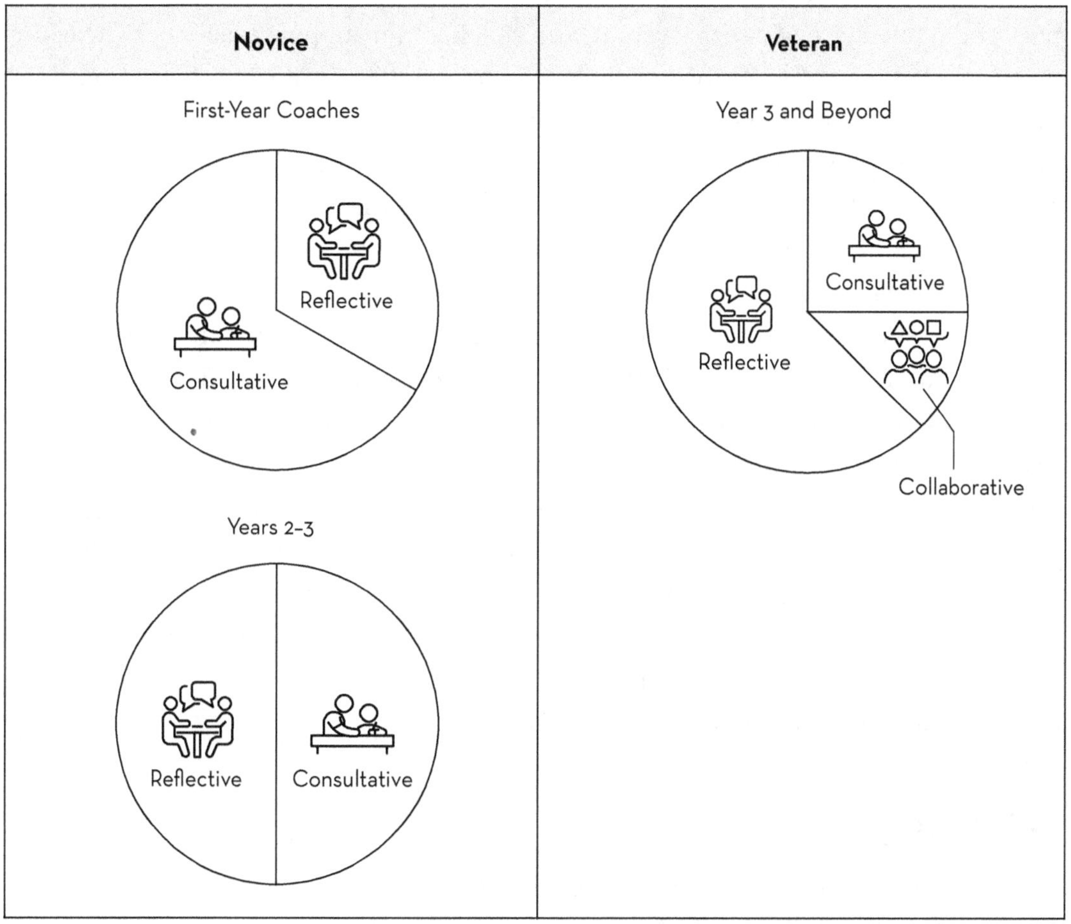

Novice	Veteran
First-Year Coaches — Reflective, Consultative	Year 3 and Beyond — Reflective, Consultative, Collaborative
Years 2–3 — Reflective, Consultative	

Teaching is highly performative work; that's why teachers are so taxed at the end of a day. They're continually thinking as they're teaching, monitoring student understanding to adjust their next step for optimal learning. This type of mental agility makes it difficult to see the larger picture. Collaborative coaching creates a space for the teacher to zoom out and see the entire field and determine which aspect of the play to perfect. The coach then employs moves that enable the teacher to practice a specific teaching strategy, using self-reflection and the coach's feedback, until the *teacher* is satisfied with their performance. Let's look at some of those moves now.

Setting Practitioner Goals

Teachers set goals formally and informally each year. Formal goals may be a part of the teacher evaluation system, and coaches can support teachers by working on those goals together. Informal goals may be mental commitments that teachers make, such as keeping their desk more organized or getting their students talking more in class. As we explore the teacher-centered models of Coaching Minicycles and the Co-Teaching Cycle (see Chapter 6), we'll see that setting a practitioner goal can be embedded into these structures. By doing so, we ensure that we're able to measure the effect of our work with teachers.

The most effective way to meet the needs of multilingual students is to set goals that focus on growing their English language proficiency. However, once we reach the collaborative level of language coaching, we're now *connecting the growth of students to teacher practice.* Setting that practitioner goal requires the teacher to be open and honest about the growth they wish to see in their teaching practice. Setting a goal with a teacher using Jim Knight's (2017) PEERS goal framework can provide guidance. These goals are designed to be Powerful, Easy, Emotionally compelling, Reachable, and Student focused. The student-focused aspect makes this framework ideal for working with multilingual students; the goal the teacher sets must have a direct effect on their students' language proficiency.

Self-Rating

In *Improving Teacher Development and Evaluation,* Robert Marzano and colleagues (2020) provide insight into transforming teacher evaluation by shifting the purpose to teacher development. Self-rating and setting goals are important parts of this work. Adult learning theory reminds us of the importance of self-concept; adult learners thrive when they can take responsibility for the learning process.

Self-rating is a reflective action requiring the teacher to measure their own practice and compare it with a specific standard or to their ideal. One of my favorite coaching questions comes from Jim Knight (2017) in his book *The Impact Cycle:* "On a scale of 1–10, with 1 being the worst lesson you've taught and 10 being the best, how would you rank that lesson?" I remember the first time I was asked the question as a teacher; it really made me pause. To answer, a teacher has to consider what they believe an excellent lesson is, and they have to reflect on what makes teaching successful. Their answer also provides insight into what the teacher values, which can help guide a coach's work.

In this space, coaches must lean into emotional intelligence, self-awareness, and partnership to be able to navigate their own emotions and avoid eroding trust by operating in judgment. Asking a teacher to self-rate means asking them to be vulnerable, to judge themselves—and, in my experience, teachers are more likely to point out what went wrong than what went right. The fact is, we live in a highly competitive and comparative society, and our minds are prone to critique, to constantly judging ourselves. Most of our self-critical thoughts take the form of an inner dialogue, a continual commentary and evaluation of what we're experiencing (Neff, 2011), and it trains our brains to see the negative in ourselves. The self-aware coach can refrain from allowing their own inner critic to drive the conversation when asking a teacher to self-rate.

When working with a teacher, it's highly possible that the things you see as excellent—or not—will differ from what the teacher points out. I had a language coaching conversation with a kindergarten teacher we'll call Ellen. Nine of her 21 students were multilingual learners at varying levels of proficiency. She reached out to me to ask what it would look like to co-teach with me in order to advance her students' writing skills. As a second-year coach, it excited me when a teacher reached out requesting to co-teach. My first step was to observe the students in the writing block to see what their needs might be.

This observation still stands out vividly in my mind. Several students roamed around, apparently unable to figure out how to sharpen their pencils; two girls had abandoned ship entirely and were off playing dolls in the cozy library corner. I had to work to smile and maintain a nonjudgmental face. After the writing block, I thanked Ellen for allowing me into her classroom, then I went to my office to reflect.

I needed to process my emotions. I took time to journal, noting only the things that went well and imagining what the teacher might be feeling with so much happening in her classroom. I realized that I admired her for allowing me into her space. That took courage. Several times during the 45-minute block, she thanked me for answering a student's question on how to spell a word or sharpen a pencil. "It's so nice having another adult in the room," she sighed. Ellen needed neither my help nor my pity; what she *did* need was a space to reflect in, one that would empower her to make her classroom one in which she and her students could thrive. To enter a space of reflection and collaboration with wisdom, we coaches must be aware of our own feelings without getting hijacked by them.

Our co-teaching cycle lasted eight weeks and taught me many lessons. Chief among them is that it takes much more effort to focus on what goes well, as opposed to what goes poorly. Our role during a rating conversation is to hold up a mirror by listening and paraphrasing. We want teachers to see their strengths reflected—initially, we call out their strengths—but the goal is for the teacher to be able to hold up the mirror themself after the coaching conversation or cycle is complete (Aguilar, 2013).

You may be wondering how we get teachers to improve their practice with this focus on strengths. A mirror shows it all, the perfectly winged eyeliner as well as the out-of-place hair. Inherent in rating a lesson, especially on a scale, is seeing both the strength and the weakness. Asking these questions can help: What would have to change to move your lesson closer to a 10? What would students be doing differently if your class rated a 10 (Knight, 2017)?

Taking this a step further, Marzano and colleagues (2020) introduce the concept of self-reflection scales. These self-rating tools provide a quantifiable standard for teachers to evaluate their proficiency in a particular teaching strategy on a scale from 1 to 4. In terms of supporting multilingual students, self-reflection scales might focus on specific linguistic scaffolds or teaching strategies, such as using sentence stems, word banks, or structured conversations. Figure 3.3 shows a self-reflection scale, this one using a rating of 1–5, that focuses on how to use sentence stems.

In addition, instructional playbooks provide checklists that make it easier for coaches to clearly describe teaching practices; they offer a "clarity that resolves resistance" (Knight, 2017, p. 108). For example, providing a step-by-step list of what it looks like to use a structured conversation can give teachers clarity and the confidence to add this new tool to their toolbox. Sharing checklists with teachers during a coaching minicycle, co-teaching cycle, or professional learning session can build teacher capacity. (See Appendix D, Instructional Checklists, for an example of a checklist to foster dialogue.) A checklist provides concrete steps of what success looks like, whereas the self-reflection tool, which teachers can use subsequent to their work with the checklist, will enable them to see how close they are to success.

FIGURE 3.3

Proficiency Scales: Sentence Stems

Target Question: How do I encourage students to speak and write in complete sentences?	
Rating 1–5	**Scale Criteria**
1	I provide sentence stems when <u>students request them</u>.
2	I provide sentence stems <u>sporadically</u>.
3	I **embed** sentence stems into lessons <u>daily or weekly</u>.
4	I embed sentence stems with **academic vocabulary** into lessons <u>daily or weekly</u>.
5	I embed sentence stems with **academic vocabulary** into lessons <u>whenever I give students speaking or writing opportunities</u>.

Journaling

In recent years, the importance of mental health awareness has become a common topic of conversation globally, as well as in the field of education. Words such as *self-care* and *mindfulness* have become popularized in an effort to improve mental health conditions. Journaling is one form of self-care that yields real results in this area. In fact, researchers suggest that expressive writing has the power to physically heal by allowing us space to organize events in our mind, giving our brains freedom to rest at night (Phelan, 2018). Coaches need to practice self-care because we cannot pour from an empty cup. Journaling after coaching conversations enables us to organize our thoughts and process them slowly so we can continually show up as the best version of ourselves.

Journaling is an act of self-awareness. It takes courage to face ourselves, which is why journaling falls under the collaborative coaching category. Without exploring what I was feeling after observing Ellen's classroom, I would not have gotten to a space where I could center on Ellen's needs. Time can often be a barrier to the practice. After a difficult, puzzling, or emotional conversation or encounter on campus, I have found it helpful to set a timer for two to five minutes and just write. If writing is not your jam, consider sketching or talking into an audio app on your smartphone, or, if you're alone, even just talking out loud to yourself. The end goal is to process, either orally or in written form, those hidden emotions that may be motivating our behavior in positive or negative ways. In *Permission to Feel*, author Marc Brackett (2020) outlines five skills that enable us to operate in emotional intelligence. He uses the acronym RULER: Recognize, Understand, Label, Express, and Regulate. Brackett writes, "These are mental skills like any others—they enable us to think smarter, more creatively, and to get better results from ourselves and the people around us" (p. 54). When we see ourselves and others more clearly, we can work more productively, putting our own bias and agendas to the side. Awareness of how and what we feel—and the implications of those feelings—makes us better collaborators.

Rehearsing

Teaching is in many ways similar to giving a presentation. It's best practice to run through a presentation before delivering it, and the same is true for teaching a lesson to students. When co-planning or engaging in a coaching minicycle with a teacher, rehearsing how to guide students into a structured conversation can create an opportunity for teachers to hone their skills. Rehearsal can feel awkward and requires a level of vulnerability, so this move may not be beneficial to every teacher and may not feel natural to every coach. However, rehearsing what it sounds like when we check for understanding or offer wait time can increase teacher confidence. This is true for novice teachers, teachers new to a grade level, or veteran teachers implementing a new teaching strategy.

Reviewing Video or Audio

As job-embedded professional development has become more widespread in education, so, too, has video become more widespread as a reflective tool. Watching a video of a classroom practice facilitates self-reflection by showing instructional strengths and gaps, creates a connection among educators, breaks down silos that naturally exist within districts, and fosters collaboration among colleagues to build collective knowledge and share coaching efforts (Spangler, 2022). When working at the collaborative coaching level, having a clear picture of reality through video is essential to developing practitioner expertise. When viewing videos of themselves teaching, teachers will inevitably notice gaps in their practice that they're intrinsically motivated to improve.

When reviewing such videos or audios, coaching happens in the self-reflection questions posed: What did you notice? What went well? How would you rate the lesson on a scale of 1 to 10? If you had to reteach this lesson right now, what's one thing you would adjust? Using videos in this way should be the teacher's choice, not one that is mandated. If a teacher is not interested in working with video, perhaps using an audio format or moving to a different self-reflection tool, such as proficiency scales, would be more agreeable. Our goal at the collaborative coaching level is to develop expertise, so the reflection tool should be fluid. As Jim Knight (2017) pointed out, "Improvement is an expectation for every professional, but people will be enthusiastic about growth when they have control over how they improve" (p. 32). We honor the professionalism of teachers and their needs as adult learners by providing safety through autonomy.

Tying It Up

In this chapter, we've unpacked the moves and practices within the framework of language coaching. By moving along the continuum of consultative, reflective, and collaborative coaching, we can amplify the effect of language acquisition strategies. As coaches and instructional leaders, we must also be strategic with our time, spending time at coaching levels in a way that enables us to widen our impact.

Mind Your Ms

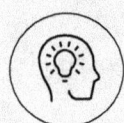

Maximize Your Motivation
- Find an emotion chart to tape into your journal, save on your smartphone, or keep in a visible space. After a difficult or puzzling coaching conversation, use the chart to name and journal about the encounter.
- Take time to focus on your inner dialogue. Consider writing down what it sounds like in a journal, on a sticky note, or on the Notes app on your smartphone. What do you notice about your inner dialogue?

Mold Your Mindset

Research and read about emotional intelligence-building resources that can grow your coaching skill set. Here are some suggestions:
- *Dare to Lead: Brave Work. Tough Conversations. Whole Hearts* (2018) by Brené Brown
- *Self-Compassion: The Proven Power of Being Kind to Yourself* (2011) by Kristin Neff
- *Permission to Feel: Unlocking the Power of Emotions to Help Our Kids, Ourselves, and Our Society Thrive* (2019) by Marc Brackett
- *Emotional Agility: Get Unstuck, Embrace Change, and Thrive in Work and Life* (2016) by Susan David

Make Your Moves
- Make a list of all the coaching behaviors and activities you have engaged with over the last week. Consider how much time you spent on each. Categorize them by consultative, reflective, or collaborative. What do you notice? What do you wonder?

- Review the three levels of language coaching—consultative, reflective, and collaborative—discussed in this chapter. Highlight the moves that come most natural to your experience, strengths, and interests. Circle the moves that may require more research, thought, and practice.

4

Student-Centered Coaching Models

"Theory is splendid but until put into practice, it is valueless." This quote, attributed to American businessman James Cash Penny, more widely known as JC Penney, is a reminder that although frameworks are important, they're useless unless we actually apply them. Theory shares the knowledge and experience of others; practice gives us our own experience. Theory is learned by taking in information, practice by *using* the information.

In this age of technology, we often place a higher premium on practical knowledge, on "hands-on learning." Of course, we can't practice well without building knowledge with theory first. It's practical knowledge, however, that leads to change. Rather than seeing these two types of knowledge as competitors, I view them as teammates in a relay.

Together, we have completed the first leg of our relay—the theory leg—in Chapters 1 through 3. Now we're passing the baton to the second leg: practice. How do we apply the frameworks we've explored? What do our core coaching beliefs look like in action? How does implementing the levels of language coaching affect teachers? How can we leverage the layers of quality language acquisition instruction in classrooms with our multilingual learners? How can we guide teachers through the steps to grow students' language proficiency as they plan and deliver instruction?

Coaching Models: An Overview

Coaches use coaching models to partner with teachers and students to support teaching and learning. A key word here is *partnership*, one of our core coaching beliefs. Engaging with students from a partnership stance means we're affirming their personhood and holding high expectations for their abilities and success. Engaging with teachers from a partnership stance means we acknowledge the teacher's expertise and are eager to learn with and from the teacher.

Ultimately, we have two goals as we coach for multilingual student success. The first is growing students' language proficiency so they reclassify as English proficient. The second goal is building the capacity of teachers to plan and deliver instruction that grows students' language proficiency so they reclassify as English proficient. Please note that our end goal is the same: to reclassify multilingual students as English proficient. To achieve these goals, we partner with both students and teachers; sometimes our partnership centers more on the student and at other times, more on the teacher. Many factors determine whether we choose a student- or teacher-centered coaching model. These include student needs and data, teacher interest and ability, and the coach's knowledge and availability. Figure 4.1 shows five coaching models.

The first two coaching models—Goal Setting and Inclusion with a Purpose—are student centered, and the final three—Collaborative Planning, the Coaching Minicycle, and the Co-Teaching Cycle—are teacher centered. All of our coaching work, whether student centered or teacher centered, should influence student learning, directly or indirectly.

This chapter will focus on student-centered coaching models. These models also provide opportunities for coaches to confer with teachers and build their theoretical knowledge. As coaches, our primary work is with teachers, so it's important that even when we're using a student-centered model, we strategically leverage opportunities to build teacher capacity.

FIGURE 4.1

Five Coaching Models

Partnering with students and teachers to support teaching and learning

Goal Setting	Inclusion with a Purpose	Collaborative Planning	Coaching Minicycle	Co-Teaching Cycle
• Focus is on offering targeted language support and raising student awareness • Uses goal-setting cycle • Serves students directly • Uses student conferences and teacher conferring to support student goal attainment	• Focus is on targeted language or content support • Uses goal-setting cycle • Serves students directly • Uses scaffolding and conferring with students during class to support student goal attainment	• Focus is on broadly increasing language-rich and linguistically scaffolded instruction • Serves students by serving teachers • Focus is on grade levels with large numbers of multilingual learners • Focus is on grade levels with multiple teachers new to serving multilingual learners	• Focus is on embedding one specific linguistically scaffolded or language-rich move into teacher praxis • Serves teachers directly • Focus is on teacher reflection on practice • Pertains to a classroom where a teacher has requested support using a specific coaching move	• Focus is on developing teacher praxis and transfer of language-rich and linguistically scaffolded instructional moves • Involves a full partnership with classroom teacher • Pertains to classrooms with large numbers of multilingual learners • Pertains to classrooms where a teacher has requested coaching for serving multilingual learners

Student-Centered Models Versus Teacher-Centered Models

Learning about Diane Sweeney's student-centered coaching framework was pivotal for me as a language coach. Sweeney (2010) notes, "The goal of school-based coaching is to improve student learning by providing continuous, relevant, and job-embedded support to teachers" (p. 7). Although I knew that all coaches should be student centered, my role with multilingual students made this idea even more crucial. The number of multilingual learners enrolling in our district far outpaced the knowledge and experience of our teachers to serve their unique needs.

Student-centered coaching means that our goal is to set and reach goals for student learning (Sweeney & Mausbach, 2018). However, both student-centered and teacher-centered methods of support are necessary to reach those goals. Here's why. In traditional pull-out programs, the classroom teacher doesn't have any connection to the language support that the student receives. As my role changed from language specialist to language coach, I became aware that teachers typically preferred the pull-out approach. Many just wanted me to pull out the multilingual students, sprinkle some English dust on them, and send them back better able to learn in English. Both student-centered and teacher-centered coaching models focus on reshaping this mindset through strategic partnership. To coach for multilingual learners' success, we must target both student language acquisition and teacher knowledge and expertise.

Figure 4.2 helps us compare student-centered and teacher-centered models more closely.

FIGURE 4.2

Student-Centered Versus Teacher-Centered Coaching Models

Student-Centered	Teacher-Centered
Coaching models in which the coach works directly with students and indirectly with teachers to grow the language proficiency of multilingual learners	Coaching models in which the coach works directly with teachers and students to grow the language proficiency of multilingual learners
Features • Focuses on growing student language proficiency • Uses consultative coaching with teachers to plan and monitor goals • Serves students directly and teachers indirectly	**Features** • Focuses on building teacher capacity to grow student language proficiency • Uses reflective and collaborative coaching to grow teacher pedagogy and practice • Serves teachers directly and students indirectly
Examples of Coaching Models Goal Setting Inclusion with a Purpose	**Examples of Coaching Models** Collaborative Planning Coaching Minicycle Co-Teaching Cycle

In student-centered models, the coach works directly with students to raise their awareness of their own affective, linguistic, and cognitive needs. Typically, the work focuses on a specific goal. The coach also works with teachers, but indirectly, on planning and monitoring those goals. With both stakeholders, the coach builds awareness and rapport that will encourage risk taking. The student is taking a risk learning a new language, and the teacher is taking a risk implementing a new strategy and thinking about language acquisition differently.

When implementing student-centered coaching models, the coach needs a firm understanding of the layers of quality language acquisition. To review, these refer to practices that are linguistically accommodated, language and literacy rich, and asset-based and equity-driven. Let's look for a moment at linguistically accommodated instruction. As the coach confers with students and teachers to set goals, many of these goals will be rooted in growing language. The coach will ensure that the student is aware of their own language proficiency and the scaffolds they have access to and knows how to request and use those scaffolds. The coach will ensure that the teacher has identified student proficiency levels and selected scaffolds. By focusing both students and teachers on identifying language proficiency and scaffolding, we have addressed the first two steps in the empowering language proficiency four-step process—learn, plan, teach, and reflect—shown earlier in Figure 2.7.

Student-Centered Model 1. Goal Setting

Goal setting as a coaching model is an opportunity to work directly with specific students to target a specific language domain. Throughout the process, we're raising student awareness of their own linguistic abilities. Students are directly involved in the selection and monitoring of their own goals, creating a sense of ownership and empowerment. Language coaches or instructional leaders monitor student progress by conferring with students regularly, and with teachers as needed.

Goal setting can also be leveraged to raise teacher and parent/family awareness of a student's linguistic needs. Of the two student-centered coaching models, goal setting is the least time-intensive to implement. The entire process can take from 4 to 12 weeks, depending on the goal, the student's rate of progress, and the amount of time the coach or leader is available to confer with students.

Before You Begin

Before beginning the goal-setting cycle with students, **review the data** to determine which students would benefit from this coaching model. Did students across the campus score lower in a particular domain on their annual standardized language assessment tests (ACCESS, ELPA21 Summative, TELPAS, or ELPAC)? Which domain do most students need support in? Is there a particular skill or standard within this domain that more students need to show growth in?

Goal setting is best implemented with multilingual learners who are at the early-intermediate to near-proficient levels of language proficiency because they have enough social English to support reflective conferring and check-ins. In addition, they can articulate their language awareness in English. I found that the speaking domain was consistently the area of our state language assessment that prevented my students from reclassifying as English proficient. Using the student goal-setting cycle was helpful in increasing awareness and targeting specific speaking skills.

Many of my students who were close to proficiency didn't even realize they were considered multilingual learners. They had been in English-speaking schools for several years, many having entered as kindergartners or 1st graders. Often their parents spoke a different language, but they were primarily English speakers. However, they didn't fully understand the purpose of the test they were taking. Taking the time to raise the students' awareness of their language proficiency levels paved half of the road to success. The other half came from setting goals and conferring.

Along with reviewing the data, I also took time to **observe students in class**. I wanted to gain information specifically on student speaking behaviors, so I popped into classes—including special periods, such as art, music, and lunch—for 5 to 10 minutes during the day. This helped me take note of both social and academic language. Observing students in different content areas also supported students who had a greater interest in a given subject area. If your focus were on writing, looking at student work samples and analyzing writing behaviors across writing genres and content would help you select a goal.

You'll also need to **decide on the scope and sequence of the goal-setting cycle**. How long will the cycle last? What action steps will students take once a goal has been set? How often will you check in with students? What will these check-ins look like? What resources will students need to monitor their own progress? How will you monitor their progress? And how will you share their progress with other stakeholders?

Finally, you must **meet with the classroom teacher**. Be sure to let the teacher know before you pop into their classroom, even if your sole focus is the student. It's imperative to not appear evaluative, and unannounced pop-ins give the impression of evaluation. I always emailed teachers beforehand to explain that I would be engaging in goal setting with their students and that I wanted to observe the students' speaking habits in class to guide our time together. I also shared when I planned to meet with the student and offered teachers the option of meeting with me in person to learn more about the student's goal. Whether they chose to meet with me or not, I always emailed a summary of the goal and a video in which the student explained the goal in their own words.

Not surprisingly, every teacher chose to watch their students' videos. This often led to teachers asking more questions or chatting about their students. Having students make these videos was strategic on my part; I wanted to compel teachers to get curious about their students' language needs. Because the students I set goals with were often at higher levels of language proficiency, language differences and needs were not always at the forefront of teachers' minds. This can often work against our end goal of reclassifying students as English proficient. Once students begin to near proficiency, they require targeted instruction to demonstrate proficiency on standardized language assessments. The time I spend conferring and goal setting with students includes having them share ways they believe their teachers can support them in class, information that I subsequently share with the teachers.

The student goal-setting cycle has four phases: conferring, setting a goal, providing support, and reflecting. Let's look at each of these in more detail.

Phase 1. Conferring

The first step in the goal-setting process is conferring, first with the student and then with the teacher. Goal-setting conferences with students can take place in small groups of four to six students or individually. A great starting point is asking the student how they view themselves as a language learner. Is the student *aware* they're a multilingual learner? If so, what does this mean to them? What do they know about their language proficiency levels? The initial goal-setting conference and the conferring check-ins that follow are all about creating a space for students to reflect on themselves as language learners.

Use this time to affirm students' cultural and linguistic heritages. The Collaborative for Academic, Social, and Emotional Learning, CASEL (Fenner & Teich, 2024), lists identifying personal, cultural, and linguistic assets as a self-awareness competency. The initial goal-setting conference sets aside time to intentionally do just that. I particularly enjoyed putting students in the teacher seat by asking them to teach me about their language. The way students' eyes light up when you validate their cultural and linguistic assets is priceless! As Fenner and Teich note, "Validating [multilingual learners'] language and culture acknowledges that, as educators, we honor what they bring with them and encourage them to maintain, as well as enhance, the gifts they bring as they acquire English and become more comfortable in U.S. culture" (p. 74). In an initial goal-setting conference, you can use the questions that follow to validate students' cultural and linguistic assets while building their self-awareness:

- Do you know what it means to be bilingual or multilingual?
- Some people believe being bilingual is a superpower. How might knowing more than one language be helpful?
- Tell me about the language you speak at home. How do you say "Good morning" in your language?
- How is the language you hear or speak at home different from or similar to English?
- We measure language competency in four areas: listening, speaking, reading, and writing. Which area is easiest for you in English? In your heritage language? Which one is most challenging in English? In your heritage language?

After discussing some of these questions with students, take time to share with them their language assessment data from the standardized test they took in the spring or any local assessments that measure language proficiency. Review the purposes of the assessment, clarifying that the goal is to score proficient (whatever that score is in your context) to reclassify as English proficient. Transparency about standardized assessments fosters academic and linguistic awareness.

Phase 2. Setting a Goal

Once students understand their current level of language proficiency, it's time to set a goal. Targeting a specific domain helps with precision in goal setting. It also provides a concrete set of skills that students can work toward.

Each U.S. state has specific skills in various domains that students must work to master. In Texas, we have the English Language Proficiency Standard, or ELPS. WIDA states—those belonging to the World-class Instructional Design and Assessment (WIDA) consortium—use their WIDA English Language Development (ELD) standards. States participating in the English Language Proficiency Assessment for the 21st Century (ELPA21) refer to their standards, whereas California uses what they refer to as English Language Development (ELD) standards. Regardless of the state, one common theme runs through all: proficiency level descriptors, or PLDs. These are a continuum of proficiency levels that describe the behaviors students might demonstrate at a given level or within that domain.

To determine which skills students should work toward, you'll need to review the standards and PLDs within your state, narrowing them down to a set of manageable student-friendly skills. Prioritizing standards is an essential part of establishing a focus on learning; we acknowledge that all standards are important but that some are more important than others (DuFour et al., 2016). In the case of goal setting, the expressive domains of writing and speaking lend themselves toward goal setting much more easily than the receptive domains of listening and reading because they're output skills that we can easily observe and measure.

Figure 4.3 displays speaking and writing skills that are ideal for students to use as goals. The science part of teaching is in researching the standards and proficiency level descriptors for your state. The art is in pairing the ideas you glean from your research, your conferences with students, and your personal beliefs. Combining the art and science will enable you to craft goals that are rooted in data, that your students will find compelling, and that you can easily measure.

The first time I engaged in goal setting, I selected a group of four 4th graders who were at the near-proficient level. My targeted domain was speaking because this portion of the standardized language assessment had prevented them from reclassifying as English proficient. I began by building their self-awareness through explaining multilingualism and inviting them to share their experiences with and observations about their heritage language and English. Next, I shared with them their language assessment scores from the spring and noted their thoughts and feelings about their proficiency levels. I then invited them to rate their current speaking behaviors using a student-friendly proficiency scale, which helps students understand the continuum of knowledge and where they are along that continuum (Marzano, 2017). This builds self-awareness. I recommend developing your own student proficiency scales by selecting a skill and three or four progressive levels toward mastery. Take into consideration your observations and what you have learned from state frameworks and standards, as well as your own professional expertise.

FIGURE 4.3

Speaking and Writing Sample Goals

Speaking	Writing
• I can speak in complete sentences while sharing information with classmates and teachers. • I can speak using complex sentences. • I can decide when to speak socially and when to speak academically. • I can speak using correct verb tenses to communicate ideas. • I can speak using plural and singular nouns correctly. • I can use academic vocabulary when explaining my thinking or justifying opinions. • I can speak using precise nouns rather than simple pronouns. • I can speak using precise verbs. • I can speak using precise adjectives.	• I can write in complete sentences while sharing information with classmates and teachers. • I can write using complex sentences. • I can write using correct verb tenses to communicate ideas. • I can write using plural and singular nouns correctly. • I can write using academic vocabulary. • I can write using precise nouns rather than simple pronouns. • I can write using precise verbs. • I can write using precise adjectives. • I can write using punctuation correctly. • I can write using various sentence lengths and patterns. • I can write using compound sentences.

Once students have rated themselves on a specific skill, it's time to brainstorm the action steps needed to reach the next level on the scale or, if you've chosen not to use proficiency scales, for the goal you selected. The first time you do this, you may find it beneficial to preselect goals rather than involve students in the process. The more versed you become in the model, the more autonomy you can give students. In terms of management, it's easier to facilitate the cycle when students have the same goal, so grouping students by goal is ideal.

Once you've determined the goal and action steps, have students record their goal in writing and orally in a video. You can share the videos not only with the students' teachers, but also with students' family members. It's helpful to show the videos to students at the end of the cycle so they can reflect on their progress.

Figure 4.4 shows sample scales that connect to common speaking and writing skills. You may choose to have students self-rate in several skills, or you may use just one if you've already decided on a given skill or goal area for the student.

Phase 3. Supporting

Having students rate themselves and name action steps makes supporting them and tracking their progress much easier. You can check in with students either weekly or biweekly, depending on the length of time you've set for the cycle. These check-ins are reflection opportunities in which you review the student's writing samples and audio or video recordings together. You might ask questions such as, Have you noticed a difference in your writing or speaking? Has the list of conjunctions been useful? The student's reflection and responses will drive the check-in. If the student feels successful, celebrate their progress. If they feel indifferent or unsuccessful, it may be helpful to set an intention or reframe success. For example, you might define success as using a single conjunction in their writing between now and the next check-in. If you think the student needs practice, set aside time to take a simple sentence from their work sample and turn it into a complex sentence. Also, after listening to an audio recording or watching a video they've completed, you both can discuss specific opportunities in the recording where they might use complex sentences. The support stage in the cycle provides opportunities for feedback, practice, and clarifying misconceptions. Feedback is a crucial aspect of learning and improving, and paired with practice, it's powerful.

Phase 4. Reflecting

At the end of the cycle, it's time to formally celebrate success. Celebration can range from offering a small but meaningful token, to awarding a certificate of

FIGURE 4.4

Sample Proficiency Scales and a Student Self-Rating

Sentence Structure Rating 1–4			
1	2	3	4
I speak/write using single words or phrases.	I speak/write using phrases or short sentences.	I speak/write using short but complete sentences.	I speak/write using both long and short complete sentences.
Academic Vocabulary **Rating 1–4**			
1	2	3	4
I am not sure which vocabulary words are academic and which ones are social.	I rarely use academic vocabulary when I explain my thinking aloud.	I only use academic vocabulary to explain my thinking aloud when my teacher gives me a sentence stem/starter or the words are on the board.	I use academic vocabulary to explain my thinking *and* I can list examples.
Sample Student Self-Rating			
Proficiency Scale Rating and Goal	**Action Steps**		
Rating: Level 3. I speak using short but complete sentences. **Goal:** I can speak using complex sentences.	• I will review complex sentences. • I will place a list of subordinating conjunctions (*because, although, since*) on my desk. • I will refer to my list during writing responses, and I will highlight the conjunctions I use. • I will refer to my list when recording responses on Seesaw and replay my response to listen for the conjunctions I use.		

recognition, to making a positive phone call home. You can compile any audio or video recordings you have of the student and share their progress with both teachers and caregivers. The student should also reflect on this compilation and celebrate their own growth. Marzano (2017) notes that proficiency scales offer two kinds of feedback: feedback on status and feedback on growth. Status celebrates where a student currently is on the scale, whereas growth celebrates the knowledge gained by the end of the cycle. This phase focuses primarily on celebrating knowledge gained. The knowledge students gained could be about complex sentences—or about themselves as language learners or learners in general. The goal-setting cycle opens the door to metacognition and invites students to think both critically and reflectively.

When we set goals with students, we implement each aspect of asset-based, equity-driven practices: relationships, relevance, and rigor. We affirm students' personal, linguistic, and cultural identities through our support and the reflection we engage in. We set relevant goals, thereby fostering student-empowered learning. And we cultivate rigor and high expectations by sharing data with students and inviting them to become active participants and independent learners.

Implementing: Questions to Consider

Having a holistic picture of a coaching model, as well as smaller action steps to take, makes implementation more effective. Appendix E, Coaching Questions for Linguistic Growth, provides questions to consider, along with steps to take throughout the cycle.

Take a moment to pause and decide if this model will work for your coaching style and context. What aspects of this model resonate with your educational philosophy or with who you are as a coach? Which aspects are supported by initiatives and systems already in place in your context? These questions are important to consider before implementing any coaching model to avoid initiative overload. As educators, we want to help, but without clear boundaries, helping can hurt. Healthy boundaries include knowing your priorities and having realistic expectations. It's also important to define success. The first time you implement goal setting, success may simply be having your students learn more about themselves. Taking time to weigh the advantages, define success, and align your priorities are great ways to set and honor boundaries.

Student-Centered Model 2. Inclusion with a Purpose

In this second model of student-centered coaching, Inclusion with a Purpose, the coach or instructional leader uses language scaffolds during class to support student goal attainment. Although the model is in direct service to students, it requires an initial conference with the classroom teacher to set a goal and discuss the logistics of in-class support.

Inclusion with a Purpose was born out of a desire for more purposeful "push-in" services for multilingual students. Historically, program models or services for multilingual students have included push-in and pull-out services. With push-in services, the language specialist goes into the classroom to support the student, whether they're a newcomer or near proficient, with independent activities and tasks. The students benefit from language support, and the teachers learn new strategies by observing the specialists working with the student (Billak, 2019). With pull-out services, the language specialist typically pulls students out from the class to provide small-group language support. This is most beneficial for newcomers or those at the beginning levels of language proficiency because it gives students targeted time to focus on English language development.

I remember the first time I pulled a group of 3rd grade newcomers. The boys were all from South Korea and had been in U.S. schools for a year or less. I had a wonderful English lesson planned that focused on the students getting to know one another using basic English sentence stems. As I pulled each student from class, I said hello in Korean. One student's eyes went wide as he asked me if I spoke Korean. "No," I replied, "but I practiced my hello." I smiled. He smiled back. By the time I picked up the third and final student and began walking back to my small office where our lessons would take place, the boys all began talking to one another in Korean. Once we reached my office, I reintroduced myself and the purpose of our time together. As I began my stellar lesson, I quickly realized that the boys just wanted to talk... in Korean.

Before pulling each student out, I had spent time observing them in class to familiarize myself with their faces and get a feel for some of their general needs. I noticed how quiet they were. They listened and followed along but rarely spoke. I thought how lonely that must feel, especially for a 9-year-old. As I tried to redirect the boys to my riveting sentence stems, they politely repeated the stem in English—then continued to speak to one another in Korean. Their smiles were what I noticed most. They laughed and smiled so much in the first few minutes of being in our small group, far more than they ever did in class. That's when it clicked. They needed time to socialize in their language, time to just be themselves. From that day forward, I set a timer for five minutes at the beginning of our sessions, and I just let them talk in Korean to one another. That experience grew my empathy and cultural competency, and it taught me that my small-group times could serve social as well as academic purposes.

Traditional pull-out and push-in services could benefit greatly from an overhaul to improve their effectiveness. Recalling the federal guidance from the "Dear Colleague Letter" (U.S. Department of Justice & U.S. Department of Education, 2015), we're charged with "avoiding unnecessary segregation of EL students." Pull-out services can become "unnecessary segregation" if we're not careful. This is not to say that small-group English language support doesn't have its place. Ayanna Cooper (2020) writes, "Although specialized language courses that are conducted separately from the general education course offerings may be necessary for a particular period of time, these courses must be designed to support overall student success" (p. 36).

For newcomers and those at the beginning levels of language proficiency, separate classes are necessary to help the students acclimate to U.S. schools and develop their English. However, once students reach the intermediate level, the focus should be on learning English in the context of content areas. We use the content as a vehicle to learn the language. This connects to the layers of quality language acquisition instruction—specifically, that we need to differentiate learning according to the students' language proficiency.

I'm suggesting that we shift from traditional, exclusive, and segregated program models to intentional and inclusive ones. Language acquisition expert Tan K. Huynh (2021) suggests we measure program models by their inclusivity. He defines *inclusivity* as models that enable multilingual learners to learn alongside their English-speaking peers and that view cultures, languages, and experiences as assets rather than roadblocks to growing language proficiency. Figure 4.5 shows the differences between traditional program models and the coaching models described here.

Alongside inclusivity is responsiveness. Despite what we call the models, the imperative is how we design and deliver them. Program models that are not responsive to student needs put student achievement at risk (Cooper, 2020). We can have the best intentions for our coaching models, but if we don't keep the real-time needs of our students in mind, then our models will be limited. Coaching models provide structures, but coaches create change.

FIGURE 4.5

Coaching Models Versus Program Models

Coaching Models	Program Models
Structured cycles of partnership with students and teachers to support teaching and learning	Teaching methods and environments to support English language development
Features • Promotes inclusivity and integration • Focus is on growing students' English language proficiency *and* building teacher capacity • Models follow a structure, sequence, or cycle of steps for the language coach or instructional leader to implement • Cyclical nature and involvement of multiple stakeholders promote responsiveness to student needs	**Features** • Less inclusive, more socially isolating and segregated • Focus is only on growing students' English language proficiency • Models teach students in English often divorced from the content area or reflecting a reduced level of rigor in the content area
Examples Goal Setting Inclusion with a Purpose Collaborative Planning Coaching Minicycle Co-Teaching Cycle	**Examples** Small-Group Push-In (K–8) Small-Group Pull-Out (K–8) English Immersion Classes (K–12)

Making the role shift and mental shift from language specialist to language coach can also be a significant part of the change needed to better serve multilingual learners. The educators responsible for the success of these students have to shift from a focus on one educator being the expert to *all* educators on campus taking a vested interest. If a specific educator is tasked with leading the charge for multilingual students, shifting from a specialist mindset to a coaching mindset supports building the capacity of all stakeholders. A specialist implies expertise; a coach implies leveraging that expertise to build the capacity of others. The title is not the issue here; our priority is the stance and the way we work. Regardless of the title, we should approach our instructional leadership with a coaching mindset.

Goal Setting and Inclusion with a Purpose

Inclusion with a Purpose uses the same goal-setting cycle as the student goal-setting coaching model. The two differ in that initial conferring in this model takes place with the teacher rather than the student. The goal is set as a collaborative effort between the language coach or instructional leader and the content teacher.

Another significant shift is in the nature of support. We avoid the term *push in* altogether and, instead, use language that draws on our desire for inclusivity. The coach or instructional leader offers support directly to the student in their content classroom two to three times each week. However, unlike forms of inclusion for students served through special education, Inclusion with a Purpose takes place for a specific duration of time. The goal drives the length and duration of time spent in class and ensures our eye is focused on developing the student as an independent learner.

It's important to note here that multilingualism is not a disability and should not be treated as such. When we treat multilingualism as a disability, it miseducates students; it's comparable to a misdiagnosis in medicine. It's a failure to see and respond to the true needs of the student—and that need is language acquisition, which we should facilitate using targeted linguistic scaffolds. The ultimate test of success with this model is, Can the student do this [goal] independently after the cycle is complete?

Before You Begin

The preparation for this coaching model is similar to that for goal setting. Begin by **reviewing students' language assessment data and content-area data**. With this model, it's important to focus on content data because the support will be provided in class during content-area instruction. The goal here could be either a language goal or a content goal, but typically it's both. In-class content serves as a vehicle to drive growth in language proficiency. Collaboration with the content teacher during conferring will solidify what type of goal is needed.

But quantitative data can only take us so far. The next step is to **view the student in class** and **review student work samples.** Observing the student in class can provide insight into the student's needs, as well as how to best meet those needs based on the classroom culture and climate. Some students are more introverted and reserved and won't want it to appear as though they're receiving this support, whereas others will walk directly over to you and ask for all the support you can provide. Again, before observing the student, it's wise to reach out to the content teacher to let them know that the student is in need of more direct linguistic support and that you'll be observing their learning behaviors and style in class.

The final step before the cycle goes in motion is to **consider potential language domain or content-area goals.** Draft a couple of goals that might be beneficial. In addition, consider the logistics. How many weeks might it take to complete this goal? How many times a week would you be able to offer in-class support? Thinking through these issues beforehand will ensure that the conferring time you spend with the teacher is as productive as possible.

Phase 1. Conferring

Inclusion with a Purpose is a student-centered model, yet much of the cycle occurs during class time. You'll be in the content teacher's space, so conferring with the teacher serves two purposes. One, it helps craft a goal that will be meaningful to the learning taking place in class. Our focus will be on using content to drive growth in language proficiency. Second, it establishes a partnership stance. Our core coaching beliefs remind us that partnership is the backbone of our relationship with teachers. We're guests in the teacher's classroom, and we want to ensure that our presence adds value. We do have a right to be there, yet we attract more bees with honey than vinegar.

Adult resistance is a real and true part of coaching. Some teachers will not be thrilled about having another adult in the room, just as some will welcome the support with enthusiasm. As coaches, we're creators of collaborative partnership. During conferring, we're thinking together with teachers about what new skills we want to see our multilingual students transfer into daily practice as independent learners.

We have three objectives as we confer with teachers that will prepare us to set a SMART goal:

1. Create space for the content teacher to reflect on the individual strengths and needs of the student.
2. Review and analyze proficiency level descriptors.
3. Share data and observations, and review student work.

As we confer, we're primarily at the consultative level of language coaching; we're serving as advocates, practicing committed listening and sharing information about students. We're dipping our toes into reflective coaching by paraphrasing, asking reflective questions, and eventually setting a goal. Conferring is an opportunity to invite the teacher to think more deeply and with a laser focus on the linguistic needs of students. Time is a precious natural resource in schools, so we want to be prepared with the information we need and the strategic questions we intend to ask.

It's helpful to begin by discussing the student's general strengths and any observations the teacher has made and then narrowing the focus to language, content strengths, or concerns. Reviewing and analyzing proficiency level descriptors are next, with their focus on specific language behaviors. In my experience, content teachers are well aware of a student's content-area performance; what's most needed is data regarding students' language proficiency. Have the proficiency level descriptors for your state available, and ask the teacher to take a few minutes to circle skills and behaviors they have observed students demonstrate in a particular domain. This is a great way to focus on the assets students bring to class, as well as to target specific skills for further development. At this point, the coach can provide quantitative data from language assessments. It may be appropriate to look at student work samples during this time as well.

The conferring conversation naturally leads into setting a goal. A key question to take into consideration is this: What skill, if developed by this student, would have the greatest effect on their ability to perform well in class? This question helps us work toward developing multilingual students as independent learners. Once we have the goal in hand, success criteria help us define and describe what it looks like when the student has met the goal; the criteria also let the coach or instructional leader gauge when the cycle is coming to a close. The final discussion point will be deciding on logistics—specifically, which days and times the coach will provide the in-class support. Figure 4.6 shows examples of goals and success criteria for each of five proficiency levels.

FIGURE 4.6

Inclusion with a Purpose: Sample Goals and Success Criteria

Proficiency Level	Goal	Success Criteria
Newcomer	Within three weeks, the student will be able to consistently transition to independent working time by using visual cues and translation devices.	• Can navigate translation tools independently • Looks around to see what others are doing or at visuals/anchor charts before requesting help
Emergent	Within four weeks, the student will be able to seek clarification on math assignments using a ring of sentence stems.	• Can repeat sentence stems • Recognizes when they're unsure of the next step • Uses classroom procedures to seek clarification from teacher or peers
Early intermediate	After six weeks, the student will be able to craft a one-paragraph quick-write using simple and compound sentences in response to the weekly prompt.	• Can identify simple and compound sentences • After three weeks, understands how to use a paragraph frame tool • Uses capitalization and punctuation correctly
Intermediate	After eight weeks, the student will be able to independently demonstrate consistent use of the correct verb tense, evidenced by samples taken from their math problem-solving notebook.	• Can identify various verb tenses • Orally explains thinking using correct verb tenses • Uses sentence stems during math journal responses
Near proficient	By the end of the earth science unit, the student will be able to craft a "Claims, Evidence, Reasoning" to explain their science reasoning using Tier 2 and 3 academic vocabulary.	• Can identify Tier 2 and 3 words correctly • Knows the definition of and how to use earth science academic vocabulary • Can define and describe claim, evidence, and reasoning • Uses or requests sentence stems and word banks to respond

Phase 2. Supporting

The coach or instructional leader's objective is to provide the necessary linguistic scaffolds that will enable the student to reach the goal. Let's look at the sample goal for a newcomer student: *Within three weeks, the student will be able to consistently transition to independent working time by using visual cues and translation devices.* This won't require much preparation. Bringing a toolkit with a whiteboard, visuals on a ring, and common sentence stems will enable you to work alongside the student as they learn to transition into independent work. On the other hand, consider the sample goal for the intermediate student: *After eight weeks, the student will be able to independently demonstrate consistent use of the correct verb tense, evidenced by samples taken from their math problem-solving notebook.* This may require you to review the math content, generate sentence stems, and bring materials to reteach verb tenses. This is where the coach is deep in the work of our third layer of quality language acquisition instruction—providing instruction that is linguistically accommodated.

Based on the student's proficiency level, the coach will use various linguistic scaffolds in class to make content comprehensible, ensure the student has opportunities to demonstrate understanding, and balance support with rigor. It should be noted that nonacademic goals can be set, such as a goal toward self-management for newcomers to support their transition into U.S. schools. This cycle is usually rather short and focuses on a specific skill that will enable the student to show courage, take initiative, and exhibit self-discipline and motivation (CASEL, 2023). Depending on the goal and success criteria, in-class support could range from two to three times per week. In-class support typically takes place during an independent learning time within the content-area block or class period. Taking time to explain your role to the student, as well as the goal that has been set, helps grow the student as an independent learner.

Collecting data, qualitative or quantitative, is important to monitor and facilitate progress toward goal mastery. Anecdotal notes are particularly useful with this coaching model because they drive your next steps and provide helpful feedback to the content teacher. The improvement in a student's quality of work over time or noticing a particular scaffold used will often spark a teacher's curiosity, prompting further reflection and conversation.

The teacher may find it helpful having another adult in the room to answer a question or offer student support. However, engaging in proactive communication is wise. Some teachers don't want coaches to answer content-related questions, whereas others welcome such participation. The rapport you've developed with the teacher will influence the type of in-class support. For example, some teachers want to know if this model could work with groups of multilingual learners. The answer, of course, is yes. Inclusion with a Purpose can work with small groups of three to six students who are focused on the same goal. If a larger group is involved, that would move the model toward a co-teaching experience, a model we'll explore in the final chapter. Many Inclusion with a Purpose opportunities often transition directly into co-teaching opportunities. After experiencing the benefit of having a coach in the classroom, many teachers want additional support for a greater number of students or want to learn how to better serve their multilingual students.

Collecting data in the course of your work can also be helpful as part of a multi-tiered system of support. If a multilingual student isn't making expected progress in a content area, is it because of language? Having anecdotal notes from a coach or an instructional leader who has language acquisition expertise can help determine whether language support or content support is needed. Note that a multilingual student can need content support unrelated to language acquisition.

Phase 3. Reflecting

The evaluate phase within Inclusion with a Purpose is continuous, but it's also constrained by the goal's time limit. Evaluating progress weekly can drive the type of support you provide throughout the cycle. In this way, evaluating and offering support are intertwined. For example, after one week of working with an intermediate student on using verb tenses in math journal responses, the coach may realize that the student can identify the correct verb tense in isolation but that the skill is not transferring into speaking or writing. To continue working toward this goal, we might plan to have the student underline the verbs in their responses the following week. We may also have the student rewatch the recording they made of their oral response during independent math stations and write down all the verbs they heard themself use.

Whichever method we use to facilitate transfer is guided by analyzing our data to determine next steps for the in-class support session. Evaluation can also include a reflective conversation with the content teacher. An in-person discussion or an email from the coach that includes the coach's thoughts on the student's progress and a request for feedback can spark reflection.

Celebration should always be a part of the evaluation process. Find a way to highlight this success to as many stakeholders as possible—to the student, teachers, administrators, and parents or caretakers. Making visible the effort it takes to grow language proficiency is a way to advocate for multilingual learners. Whether the student met the goal or not, celebration is in order because they made some kind of progress. What success criteria *did* the student meet? Did they develop other skills during the cycle? Not every cycle will end with a bull's-eye, and that's OK. Learning took place. The student grew in awareness or independence, and the content teacher is now more aware of their needs. Not to mention that each cycle gives us the opportunity to fine-tune our coaching practice. At the end of a cycle, take some time to reflect. What did you learn about yourself as an educator and a coach? What worked well during this cycle? What would you do differently next time? Why? As the saying often attributed to John Dewey goes, "We do not learn from experience—we learn from reflecting on experience."

Implementing: Questions to Consider

What resonates with you in this coaching model? What aspects seem attainable and beneficial? What roadblocks do you foresee? Do the potential benefits make the roadblocks worth overcoming? Why or why not? How does this model align with your coaching beliefs and goals? What would success look like if you implemented this model? Does this align with your priorities? With the priorities of your campus?

We've now looked at two student-centered models of coaching. You can use the following questions to help you decide which model to use:

- Does the model align with the goals of the campus?
- Do student data support a need for this type of model?
- What data would support this model?
- Based on my current reality, which model can I commit to implementing well?

Tying It Up

In this chapter, we began the second leg of our race, the practice leg. By delving into the two student-centered coaching models, we've considered what our core coaching beliefs and levels of language coaching might look like in practice. These models focus on growing multilingual students' language proficiency through directly working with students to raise their awareness of their own affective, linguistic, and cognitive needs. The coach partners with teachers to ensure the goals set will grow language and content simultaneously, and in ways that support the student as an independent learner. As the coach directly supports students, they ensure that linguistic scaffolds make content comprehensible and provide opportunities for students to show what they've learned. These models address our responsibility to identify and respond to the needs of multilingual learners by providing scaffolds to ensure their meaningful participation in the educational environment.

Mind Your Ms

Maximize Your Motivation
- Consider theory and practice. Take time to journal your response. Which one is most important? Why? Which one comes most naturally to you?
- Visit casel.org to explore the fundamentals of social-emotional learning. What do you notice? What do you wonder?

Mold Your Mindset
- Write a comparison of the two student-centered models.
- Research and read about student-centered supports to grow your coaching skill set. Here are some suggestions:
  - *Leading Student-Centered Coaching: Building Principal and Coach Partnerships* (2018) by Diane Sweeney and Ann Mausbach
  - *And Justice for ELs: A Leader's Guide to Creating and Sustaining Equitable Schools* (2020), by Ayanna Cooper

Make Your Moves
- Review the sample goals provided in this chapter; rewrite them, refining them to match your educational context.
- Review and annotate the proficiency level descriptors provided by your state.

Coaching Through Collaborative Planning

The 5th grade team had the highest number of multilingual learners on my campus. Each homeroom teacher had six to seven of these students, with four newcomer multilingual learners in the grade level. Science was an essential grade to target for linguistically diverse students because of its domain-specific vocabulary and deep content strands. Not to mention the fact that in my home state of Texas, 5th graders had to take a standardized test in the subject. I had never taught 5th grade science before; it would be an opportunity for me to learn and lean into the partnership principles with both the grade-level team and my potential co-teacher, Ms. Lott.

On this particular day, the 5th grade science teachers would be planning a unit to teach for the next two weeks. I had been in countless team plannings as a 1st grade teacher and in departmentalized plannings as a 3rd grade math and science teacher. But attending planning as a coach was different. The challenge was to be helpful while not detracting from the team agenda and workflow. How would I participate in the lesson planning when I wasn't a member of the team of science teachers? How could I balance being supportive with not being too opinionated and disrupting team synergy?

Before the session, I preplanned by reviewing their scope and sequence, pacing guides, and the district-provided science lessons so I would be prepared to serve as a thinking partner. Gathering my computer and notebook, I headed toward the 5th grade pod with questions swirling in my head. What did it look like to promote language acquisition strategies in a way that was actionable for teachers? Would they even want to hear what I had to offer? I thought that perhaps during this first meeting, I should just be a listener.

The Coach's Role in Planning

In the yesteryear of education, teachers planned lessons in isolation based on their own knowledge or interests and considering state standards and district curricula. In the 1960s, researchers began using the term *professional learning communities* (PLCs), which was perceived as "an alternative to the isolation endemic to the teaching profession in the United States" (Solution Tree, 2023). According to Richard DuFour and colleagues (2020), professional learning communities

- Ensure high levels of learning for all students.
- Work collaboratively and take collective responsibility.
- Develop a results orientation, continually seeking evidence and indicators of student learning.

The responsibility to ensure high levels of learning for all students is not—and never has been—a one-person job. The responsibility for growing the language proficiency and content knowledge of multilingual students must also be collective. We shouldn't expect that a language coach or specialist can achieve this alone or that a classroom teacher can embed linguistic scaffolds into instruction without support. Rather, we must build the capacity of all stakeholders to serve all students.

Principals, administrators, and instructional coaches should all have general knowledge of best practices and strategies for teaching multilingual learners. The language acquisition coach or specialist on campus who has deep knowledge on how to best support linguistic growth shouldn't be the only one using this knowledge to advocate for students. When a variety of instructional leaders advocate best practices for multilingual students, we see greater gains in their language acquisition, proficiency, and overall academic success (Dove & Honigsfeld, 2017).

In reference to students, I often hear educators say, "They have to Maslow before they can Bloom"—that is, that we need to meet students' basic needs on Maslow's hierarchy of needs before trying to move them into the higher-order thinking heights of Bloom's Taxonomy. One "need" that traditionally marginalized students experience is the need for safety. As Hammond (2014) noted, "It becomes imperative to understand how to build positive relationships that signal to the brain a sense of physical, psychological, and social safety so learning is possible" (p. 45). Our brains can't learn under stress. If our students feel unwelcomed or believe that others perceive them as a burden or an afterthought because they haven't yet acquired English, then our classrooms and schools become unsafe. We can create psychological safety for linguistically diverse students by raising our own awareness and leaning into the work of learning how to best advocate for all students.

As instructional leaders, we can begin by leveraging the coaching model of collaborative planning, the broadest of the models we'll explore. It involves directly working with teachers to indirectly affect students, and it's a way to work with multiple teams. In an elementary setting, it might be attending each grade level's literacy planning or attending only the grade-level planning of the team you intend to work with. At the secondary level, it might be attending each department's collaborative planning or only the collaborative planning of a department in which there are many multilingual learners who would benefit from targeted linguistic scaffolds embedded into instruction.

History is one such content area that could benefit from scaffolds, particularly for multilingual students who are new to the United States or at the beginning stages of language proficiency. The background knowledge required of history courses can make instruction in this subject more challenging. Across all grade levels and content areas, strategically collaborating with teams of teachers who serve a large number of multilingual students makes for a wider impact.

DuFour and colleagues (2016) explain how to develop a culture of collaboration: "The purpose of collaboration—to help more students achieve at higher levels—can only be accomplished if the professionals engaged in collaboration are focused on the right work" (p. 59). It's not enough for teachers to sit around a table and list the topics they will teach; they must focus on work that affects instruction. Discussing the "how" more than the "what" leads to rich conversations that grow teachers' instructional practice.

To more fully meet the needs of linguistically diverse students, we also have to focus on the "how." How does it look for the science teacher to preteach vocabulary? How can the U.S. history teacher build the needed background knowledge for a multilingual learner who didn't receive their elementary education in the United States and therefore has little knowledge of basic U.S. history? How does the 3rd grade teacher provide opportunities for students to speak and practice language during the writing lesson? Discussing linguistic scaffolds that use content to increase language proficiency is the "right work" for instructional leaders to engage in as they coach through collaborative planning.

Matching Coaching to a Team's Stage

Team dynamics play an important role here. How long has the team been working together? How do they run their meetings? Bruce Tuckman's (1965) stages of teaming provide insight into how teams develop and build their ability to work interdependently to reach their goals. He refers to the stages as *forming*, *storming*, *norming*, *performing*, and *adjourning*. The manner in which a coach engages with a team should be differentiated, based on such dynamics.

In Chapter 3, we unpacked the levels of language coaching—consultative, reflective, and collaborative—that inform how we might partner with individual teachers. By aligning the stages of team development with the levels of coaching, we can interact with teams in ways they're ready to receive. Figure 5.1 shows Tuckman's five stages of team development, with the pertinent level of language coaching noted beneath each one. Let's now consider how a coach could engage with a team in each of those stages.

Forming

Forming describes that August feeling! Teachers are returning from summer break refreshed, energized, and ready to embark on another year of teaching. They have had time to unwind and are likely infused with new ideas they're eager to implement. Some are returning teachers, but others are new to the district or campus, or to the teaching profession itself. The excitement is palpable. Each teacher has expectations. Teams begin connecting and getting to know one another, often engaging in team-building activities. Ideally, teams have time to establish how they plan to work, setting norms and collective commitments in line with serving students. This can extend through the first month or two of school, depending on both the campus culture and the team.

FIGURE 5.1

Stages of Teaming

Consultative		Reflective	Collaborative	
Forming	Storming	Norming	Performing	Adjourning
• Excitement • Anxiety • Expectancy • Small talk • Surface-level politeness • Focus on defining goals and processes	• Conflict • Responding to differences • Frustration • Clarity of purpose • Bids for power • Focus on refining roles and redefining goals	• Consensus • Flexibility • Inclusivity • Clear roles • Commitment to team vision and goals • Focus on productivity, individually and collectively	• Enthusiasm • Constructive criticism • Delegation • Clear vision • Camaraderie • Celebration • Focus on continuous improvement	• Conflicting feelings • Sadness • Anxiety • Satisfaction • Recognition • Focus on transitioning well

It's best to ground this stage in consultative coaching. You're not a member of the grade-level team but a guest. Team members are typically polite and engage in small talk as they get to know one another personally and professionally, so entering that space with an agenda could be seen as off-putting. Practice committed listening and witness the good to build trust and maintain rapport. Witnessing the good means affirming instructional and language-rich strategies. Committed listening means providing a book or resource that the teacher has said they need. See a need, fill a need. This goes a long way in the first weeks of school when there are more tasks than time.

Storming

The second phase, *storming*, is characterized by conflict, power moves, and sometimes disappointment. Not all teams will storm, especially if they've had the time and resources to fully bond. Storming might begin once a newly formed team has settled in and that August feeling has waned. If teams storm, it's likely because of differences of opinion or simply the realization that working as a team is difficult. This may leave a team feeling disenchanted at best and disgruntled at worst.

This is the stage where the team norms that were set initially are put to the test. One team norm may be "Start and end on time." But now that team members know one another, it's easier for planning sessions to stray off topic. Another norm may ask members to "Be solution-focused." But the new teacher struggling with classroom management or the returning teacher who hasn't bought into a new campus initiative might be having a hard time focusing on a solution.

Personal agendas can often emerge during this stage. This is where the team leader or department head may have to put their conflict resolution and soft skills into action. The team approach to managing conflict will determine how long this stage lasts. If an instructional leader or administrator is responsible for coaching teams, this staff member may need to partner deeply with a storming team.

The work of a coach championing multilingual students remains at the consultative level with a storming team. The best approach is to maintain any rapport built during the team's forming stage by consistently being a committed listener, resource provider, and witness to the good. If you're partnering for deeper impact with an individual teacher on a storming team, you may be able to float along the continuum between consultative and reflective. You could be co-planning and reviewing student work with that teacher if you're serving students in their class with a more robust coaching model, such as Inclusion with a Purpose or Co-Teaching.

However, the stage of the team can also have an effect on a teacher's willingness and ability to partner with you. Teachers who are on teams at the storming stage often respond to coaching in either of two ways. Either the teacher will turn deeper into partnership with the coach to maintain productivity and success with their students or become so preoccupied with the conflict on the team that they're prevented from engaging as a full partner. If the teacher turns toward deeper partnership, the coach can be reflective and even collaborative. If the teacher is unable to fully partner, then maintaining consultative coaching practices with a dash of reflective elements would be the best plan. This means continuing to provide resources but also keeping the focus primarily on the students through progress monitoring by asking the teacher student-centered questions. Practice committed listening, paraphrasing, and reflective questioning to create a space for the teacher to be heard and have a thinking partner. The goal for teachers and coaches is student success. A storming stage can slow this down, but it doesn't need to come to a complete stop. Matching the level of coaching support to the team's stage honors their current reality.

Norming

The *norming* stage transitions a team from conflict to cooperation, provided they have managed the conflict well. Rather than feeling like individuals with separate agendas, they're now able to resolve differences. The team goes from a "my students" to an "our students" mentality. They have redefined roles, revealed their individual strengths, and leaned into the good of the whole team and all the students they serve. Collective efficacy blossoms during this stage as teachers trust one another and begin to believe they can achieve more together than apart.

Serving a norming team typically grounds us in reflective coaching. You'll spend much more of your time questioning teachers and monitoring student progress. For example, if a teacher suggests building vocabulary knowledge by having students write out definitions, you might ask, How did students respond to that activity previously? A question like this takes the focus back to student outcomes and enables the teacher to evaluate how a previous activity affected student learning. Or you might ask, What do we want students to be able to do with the definitions or vocabulary words? How will we know if the students understood the definitions, and how will we measure that understanding? Questions that require us to check for understanding and define mastery are key to ensuring that we're planning meaningful instruction.

In another instance, a teacher might be hesitant to add an opportunity for a structured conversation because students often veer off topic. You might ask, How familiar are students with the topic they're discussing? Would a timer or a sentence stem keep them on topic? By asking questions like these, you can share information while focusing the teacher on what they can do to get the engagement they desire. Asking a reflective question while presuming positive intent is a powerful tool.

Performing

A *performing* team is characterized by enthusiasm and camaraderie. They not only have reached consensus but also are clear on their vision and feel safe enough to give and receive constructive criticism. The team's ability to move as one increases their effectiveness; they're truly experiencing the reality of doing more together than they ever could apart.

With a high-performing team, a language coach can be firmly rooted in reflective coaching to grow their practice. A high-performing team will stretch you. These teacher teams are usually innovative and data-informed, and they go deep into the work of instruction and student achievement. When planning with a performing team, reviewing student work, providing feedback, and engaging in data analysis are all coaching behaviors you can implement. These teams may solicit feedback because they're committed to continuously improve. When working with a performing team, as with all teams, be prepared and follow through; not doing so will erode trust.

When providing feedback focused on linguistic instructional strategies, you could use the notice and wonder phrasing (Dove & Honigsfeld, 2017):

- I noticed you all have planned a written response. I'm wondering if students could benefit from orally rehearsing their response before writing.
- I noticed more than half of the students did not answer the question correctly. I wonder what background knowledge they might need to be successful.
- I noticed the text has a lot of domain-specific vocabulary. I wonder if preteaching the vocabulary might help striving readers and those at the beginning level of language proficiency access the text.

Noticing and wondering enable you to make an observation *paired with a solution*. Teachers and teams can resist a critique if it isn't followed by a viable solution. Noticing and wondering provide a language structure to hold yourself accountable for being solution-focused. This is key when working with any team, particularly with a performing team that values effectiveness.

Adjourning

This stage was not part of Tuckman's original theory; he added it years later. It's an important and often underestimated stage that focuses on ending well. This transition phase can bring up a range of feelings, from sadness or anxiety to satisfaction. It's important to "give people their flowers" by celebrating the successes of the team and reflecting on all they accomplished. End-of-year team reflections can serve as a springboard for the following year when teams return to the forming stage. As a coach, find ways to thank teams or individuals personally. You might write a handwritten note and place it in their school mailbox. This communicates that you see and value their contributions.

Coaching Moves: Reflecting and Resourcing

We've established the "right work" of collaborative planning and how to work based on the team's stage. Now we must build our toolbox with strategies that will enable us to maximize the time we spend in collaborative planning meetings.

Take a minute to imagine your ideal planning session. Use the following questions to guide your thinking. You might journal about this or simply make a list. Lean back and ponder, close your eyes, and let yourself imagine the following:

- What are you doing?
- What are you saying?
- What are the content teachers doing?
- What are the content teachers saying?
- What makes your planning effective?
- How can you tell you're effective?
- What effect does your presence have on teacher knowledge? How do you know?
- What effect does your participation have on student learning? How do you know?

A coach may be invited to a planning meeting because a team may have raised a specific concern regarding their multilingual students. A coach could also decide to support a grade-level team or department because of the presence of a large number of multilingual students. During collaborative planning, it's crucial to offer two coaching moves: reflecting and resourcing. Reflecting supports the core coaching belief of communication, whereas resourcing supports the core coaching belief of partnership. Figure 5.2 teases out the coaching moves in each category.

FIGURE 5.2

Coaching Moves for Collaborative Planning

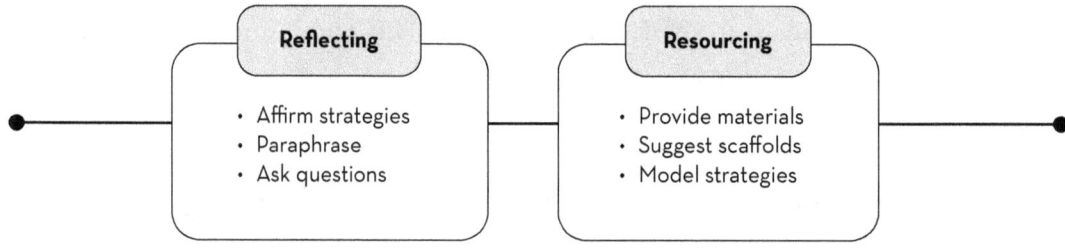

Reflecting

A quick definition search of the word *reflecting* reveals two ideas. The first has to do with sending energy back and the second, with thinking carefully. When we use reflection as a coaching move during lesson planning, we create space for teachers to think deeply by sending their thoughts back to them through affirmation, paraphrasing, or questioning. Reflecting during collaborative planning focuses on creating a space where teachers can pause and consider the instructional strategies they're using. Why are we using them? Are they effective? How do we know?

We **affirm instructional strategies** with value statements that name and acknowledge the strength of the work. For instance, "I see you're planning to provide a structured conversation after the video clip. I think that will really help you assess if the students understood the central message," or "I like that you're getting students up and moving with a graffiti wall after reading the passage. Interaction and movement help them retain information." Affirming with value statements enables us to witness the good and connect great instructional work to best practices for multilingual learners.

As social creatures wired for connection, educators like to be affirmed, and they like knowing that the decisions they're making will benefit students. This is especially true for content teachers who may not have a lot of experience or confidence teaching multilingual students, teachers who resist coaching, or those who have a deficit-based mindset regarding multilingual students. Teaching, like other service-oriented careers, is rife with feelings of underappreciation. Teachers can often feel that campus or district administrators don't understand the weight of all the tasks they must complete. This sentiment can often be extended to coaches who are no longer in the classroom. That's why affirming feedback from a coach helps create connection and builds trust; it's witnessing the good. Witnessing the good is not merely celebratory, reserved only for public moments of shout-outs during staff meetings or newsletters, although these have their benefits as well.

Affirming instructional strategies is also a way of providing feedback, a strategy at the reflective coaching level. As Marzano and colleagues (2020) explain, "Feedback tells teachers if their efforts are actually developing expertise" (p. 39). By affirming, we provide positive insight that enables teachers to become aware of the progress they're making toward providing effective instruction for multilingual students. To cultivate such language-rich classrooms, teachers must not only know the strategies but also implement them. If these strategies are new to them, teachers will be hesitant, so when we notice they're using practices that support multilingual learners, it's essential to affirm them. Raise what you praise! A principal I worked with often used this mantra regarding leadership. What we affirm we encourage; whatever we praise as quality actions is what we're raising up as the standard. Our standard is using scaffolded instruction to develop the language proficiency of multilingual students, so this is what we must affirm. We raise what we praise!

Paraphrasing during collaborative planning or even in one-on-one coaching conversations is beneficial because it lets the speaker hear their ideas aloud, an audio mirror of sorts. Author Kathy Kee and colleagues (2010) write, "The purpose of the paraphrase is not as much for the listener as it is for the benefit of the speaker. It reflects the content (and emotions) back to the speaker for consideration and connects the response to the flow of the emerging conversation" (p. 107). This reminds us that the coach's role is often most succinctly defined as a *thinking partner*. Paraphrasing is a gift to the speaker, to the teachers we serve. It enables a more connected conversation by communicating our genuine desire to understand the speaker's perspective. When I paraphrase during a coaching conversation, the speaker will often confirm or clarify their statements. Hearing our words repeated provides a chance to reorganize or solidify the ideas that can swirl in our brains. As we collaboratively plan with teachers, paraphrasing lets us know that we understand the teacher's perspective and can now determine our next move. We might affirm the instructional strategy they describe, ask a clarifying question, or move into resourcing. Whichever move we make is now more informed because we have taken the time to gain clarity.

Because coaches aren't always involved in day-to-day classroom interactions (unless you're implementing a student-centered coaching model), it's important to say to teachers, "You know your students and classroom environment best." Acknowledging this creates equality, an important partnership principle according to coaching guru Jim Knight (2022), who notes, "When coaches work from the principle of equality, collaborating teachers feel seen, valued and respected and believe they are afforded the status they deserve as professionals" (p. 20). Teachers are thinking professionals who make multiple instructional decisions in minutes as they take in a multitude of data from their students. Honoring the intense thinking work they do in the classroom or the issues they raise during planning means taking time to gain clarity. Clarity comes from listening so well that we can offer a paraphrase that creates a safe space of connection as thinking partners. When the teacher clarifies their ideas, the coach is then able to ask a reflective question.

Questioning is a powerful tool. Appendix E, Coaching Questions for Linguistic Growth, lists a variety of questions sorted according to six student outcomes or linguistic growth areas desired. These include such outcomes as encouraging comprehensible input, addressing the quality of student work, and supporting general scaffolding. You'll notice that the questions are open-ended. For example, Do students have enough background knowledge to complete this task? How can we make this text accessible to all levels of learners? or, How can we embed visuals into this lesson? Such questions create a reflective space. Because we're committed to continuous improvement and collective efficacy, we believe that teachers usually have the answers to these questions within them; they simply need the time, space, and opportunity for them to be drawn out. Elena Aguilar (2013) reminds us, "The great majority of the questions we ask in coaching should be probing questions, given that, at its broadest, our work is to help another person deepen reflective capacities and become more self-aware" (p. 159). When considering coaching for multilingual learners, we want teachers to become more self-aware of how they're designing lessons and how those lessons affect the language development and academic growth of multilingual learners. Developing lessons that are adequately scaffolded while simultaneously challenging takes thoughtful consideration. The coaching moves we employ during planning with teachers create space for them to consider how to bring these lessons into fruition.

Several weeks into the school year, I finally fell into a groove with the 5th grade science team. As we reviewed a recent common formative assessment, it became clear that students were struggling to distinguish between reflections and refractions. More than half of the grade level answered the assessment question incorrectly. "What do all the incorrect responses have in common? Any trends?" asked the science lead, Mrs. Mendoza. The team began chiming in their observations and assessments. "They're mostly one-sentence responses." "They give no scientific evidence." I posed the question "How could we use examples of short-constructed responses to help students better understand what we expect of them?" I paused and held my breath.

"What if we wrote four different examples and then had the students read them?" asked Ms. Lott. I released my breath, beginning to truly believe that maybe the co-teaching cycle with Ms. Lott was paying off. "We should have them rate the examples," said Mrs. Mendoza. "I like that! It will really get them thinking!" another teacher chimed in. "And after they rate them, they could turn and share their thinking with a partner before reading the next example. We've been trying to add more time for students to talk in our lessons," added Ms. Lott. The teachers began tossing around ideas, and I offered to make a quick QSSSA (see Appendix C) template to guide their structured conversation during the lesson.

The power of a question never ceases to amaze me. Although Appendix E lists many questions, I would caution against printing them off and asking them interview style during a planning session—not if you want to stay in the room, that is. Instead, try internalizing a couple of questions based on the needs you notice in a particular grade level. Of course, having a printout of these questions in your planning binder to reference as you attend planning sessions could be helpful. The key is remembering that your primary focus is to create a space or an opportunity for teachers to reflect as they plan.

Resourcing

This move provides teachers with **material or information** they can use during lesson delivery to meet students' instructional needs. Resourcing is important because it fulfills a tangible need of teachers and students. Teachers shouldn't see the coaching role as purely philosophical, with no practical application. As I planned with the 5th grade team, I listened to the comments they shared and noticed they wanted students to discuss their ideas with peers. So, I offered to provide a QSSSA digital template as a resource to facilitate that discussion. By providing resources, we take one thing off the teacher's plate and truly demonstrate servant leadership.

Coaches can also suggest **helpful scaffolds** (preteaching vocabulary, offering wait time, providing visual or verbal cues, and so on); these are central to increasing language proficiency. Because the 5th grade team had commented that coaches and instructional leaders who sat in on plannings often spoke too much during planning, I didn't take resourcing as far as I could have. For example, after suggesting the QSSSA, I could have added, "I'm thinking of including a word bank for some of our students at the beginning and intermediate levels of language proficiency. What academic vocabulary do you want students to use in the sentence stem?" This scaffold draws attention to academic vocabulary and gives students a way to use it with a word bank. Instead, I saved that for my co-planning session with Ms. Lott. Now, even if teachers don't implement the scaffold or instructional routine you suggest, you're raising awareness about best practices for multilingual learners. By naming the scaffold, the specific students it will benefit, and how it will benefit those students, you're building teacher knowledge of best practices for multilingual learners.

Modeling strategies is another way to share information with teachers that can influence lesson delivery. Showing a real-time example of what a linguistic scaffold may look and sound like increases the likelihood that teachers will implement it. During my time with 5th grade, I provided the resource of a QSSSA template because I had modeled this strategy during professional learning with the whole staff. Had I not done so, I could have offered to model it in one of the teacher's classrooms, send teachers a video clip of me using it with Ms. Lott's class, or even demonstrate it during the planning session right then and there.

Asking teachers to provide students with a word bank can feel like one more thing for them to do. This is when we pair suggesting a scaffold with providing the physical resource. In a planning session, I would often type the word bank or the set of sentence stems directly on the team plans or email them to the team right after planning. By taking that task from their mental load and providing the resource, teachers were more likely to use the scaffold. Eventually I noticed word banks popping up in classrooms during other lessons. The greatest reward was having a teacher stop me in the hallway and say, "My kids are asking for word banks all the time now, and it really does help their writing sound so much better!" Sometimes people have to see it before they can "see it"; modeling provides that sight.

Preparing for Collaborative Planning

Collaborative lesson planning is the space where educators huddle up; it's our practice, with lesson delivery the big game. We have to make the most of it. Before entering any planning session with a team or teacher, be sure to

- **Familiarize yourself with student data.** At what level of language proficiency are students currently performing? Which language domain is the strongest? In which language domain is growth needed? What is overall student performance like in each subject area? How often are students speaking in class? Knowing the overall proficiency levels and performance trends of students will help determine which linguistic scaffolds will be most effective.
- **Review the lesson plans**. When we review lesson plans, we're determining points in the lesson that may not be accessible to multilingual students. What are the language demands? Are students expected to speak or write? Can sentence stems, paragraph frames, or word banks aid students in constructing an oral or a written response? How much listening or reading is required? Is the text or media at a level that the students can understand? If not, how can we adapt the text or video to enable greater comprehensible input?
- **Select two to three resources or scaffolds that fit the lesson.** The goal is to provide linguistic support that reduces language barriers so students

understand the content. We can measure this understanding based on student output. Was the student able to respond when given an opportunity to share with a partner or when recording a response on a digital platform? As we pre-plan, it's imperative to raise lots of questions to dissect the lesson and potential learning experience.

- **Keep in mind team dynamics, and adjust your approach accordingly.** If we've done due diligence in unpacking the lesson using a linguistic lens, we'll have multiple entry points to offer support during planning with teams. These will also enable us to adapt our approach, depending on the team dynamic or how the planning session unfolds.

Tying It Up

In this chapter, we've defined the "right work" of a coach during collaborative lesson planning: promoting instructional strategies and linguistic scaffolds that use content to increase language proficiency. Attention to team dynamics informs the level of coaching we provide, enabling us to engage productively with a team. Finally, we explored specific coaching moves to leverage in collaborative planning that help us create a space of reflection, as well as opportunities to provide resources. By strategically preparing for collaborative planning, coaches can build the capacity of teachers to serve multilingual students.

Mind Your Ms

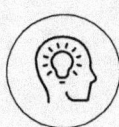

Maximize Your Motivation
- Review the Stages of Teaming graphic shown in Figure 5.1. Consider where each team on your campus or each team you work with might fall. Brainstorm two or three ways you can show up as a servant leader to partner with them.
- For teams in the storming stage, write down each team member's strengths. Before meeting with this team, review the list. This will enable you to enter the space better able to make positive presuppositions as you communicate.

Mold Your Mindset
- Research and read about collaborative planning supports to grow your coaching skill set. Here are some suggestions:
  - *Learning by Doing: A Handbook for Professional Learning Communities at Work* (2016), by Richard DuFour and colleagues
  - *The Art of Coaching Teams: Building Resilient Communities that Transform Schools* (2016), by Elena Aguilar
  - *Co-Planning: Five Essential Practices to Integrate Curriculum and Instruction for English Learners* (2021), by Andrea Honigsfeld and Maria Dove

Make Your Moves
- Rate your current reality during collaborative planning using the self-rating tools shown in Appendix A, Self-Rating Tools A–C. These tools focus on committed listening, paraphrasing, and questioning.
- Review the questions listed in Appendix E, Coaching Questions for Linguistic Growth. Choose one question from each subtopic to internalize. Be sure to rephrase the question in a way that matches your coaching voice.

Teacher-Centered Coaching Models

In teacher-centered coaching models, the coach or instructional leader partners directly with teachers to grow teacher praxis in delivering linguistically accommodated instruction. Although these models directly work to build teacher capacity, the purpose of doing so is student growth. Reflective coaching is the primary level of language coaching used here; the coach is heavily focused on creating a space conducive to thinking together.

In this chapter, we'll look at two teacher-centered coaching models: Coaching Minicycles and Co-Teaching Cycles. Both involve embedding instructional moves into lesson plans and then reflecting on that implementation. The focus is on co-planning and reviewing student work, as well as on collaborative coaching moves, such as setting practitioner goals and self-rating. We define success with teacher-centered coaching models by the effect they have on teachers and students. As author and consultant Peter Block writes, "Start measuring your work by the optimism and self-sufficiency you leave behind" (Aguilar, 2013, p. 245). As coaches and leaders, we're after impact; we want to grow people. Leaving optimism and increased confidence in serving multilingual learners in our wake is a great measure of impact.

Coaching Minicycles

Minicycles are opportunities to directly work with teachers to embed a specific linguistic scaffold, instructional move, or engagement strategy into a lesson. Coaching in this way is "focused on developing thin slices of behavior through focused observation and targeted feedback" (Marzano et al., 2020, p. 32). By doing so, we create an attainable and low-lift opportunity to grow 1 percent better. We focus on two areas in this coaching mode: reflection and transfer. Minicycles provide a structure for teachers to engage in self-reflection, which coaches or instructional leaders cultivate through reflective questioning and focused feedback. In terms of teacher transfer, we look at whether the linguistic scaffold, instructional move, or engagement strategy has become an autonomous part of the teacher's praxis. Are they able to independently embed the move into lesson planning and execute it during lesson delivery easily and fluently (Marzano et al., 2020)?

Minicycles can last between two to four weeks. They require co-planning, one or two co-taught lessons, and follow-up for the teacher to reflect on transfer. This model is ideal for teachers who are seeking to embed a specific strategy into their practice. A cycle can result from a discussion during team or department collaborative planning, a teacher requesting to work with you, or consultations you've had with a teacher on the needs of their students. Minicycles are less intense than co-teaching cycles; they're more targeted and focus more on the teacher than on the student.

I first learned about minicycles at a student-centered coaching workshop hosted by author and educational consultant Diane Sweeney. The idea of using shorter cycles to produce an effect was intriguing. Many of the language coaches I served worked across two campuses, and the longer co-teaching cycles, although beneficial, were not altogether feasible for them. Using the structure of minicycles and adapting them for the specific needs of multilingual students broadened their effect.

Longer co-teaching cycles sound more intimidating and time-consuming at the outset. If teachers are unfamiliar with coaching or the coach has not had the time to establish trust and rapport with teachers, they may be reluctant to engage in these more intense and collaborative forms of coaching. Moreover, moves at the collaborative level require a greater degree of emotional intelligence and self-awareness on the part of the coach or instructional leader. A coach must be able to navigate adult reluctance and resistance; to engage teachers in ways they're open to receiving, they must also be emotionally agile and creative. Minicycles can engage teachers while not overwhelming them. They expose teachers to the philosophy of coaching and can interest them in shifting into longer cycles or a more intense co-teaching cycle (Sweeney & Harris, 2020).

Before You Begin

Just as with student-centered models, teacher-centered models benefit from preparation. Before engaging in a coaching minicycle, begin by analyzing student data, observing students in class, and attending collaborative planning meetings. Analyzing language and content assessment data ensures we have an idea of the general needs of students before we meet with the teacher; it also helps clarify student proficiency levels and which scaffolds are most appropriate for which students. Observing students in class provides qualitative data that assessment data cannot reveal. The focus on data analysis and student observation contributes to developing a minicycle that grows teacher practice and student language proficiency. Finally, attending collaborative team planning will clarify how teachers typically select and embed scaffolds into lessons. Taking these matters into consideration *beforehand* demonstrates both effort and competency—and competency builds trust.

The minicycle follows the four steps to the empowering language proficiency process that we described earlier in Chapter 2 (see Figure 2.7): learn, plan, teach, and reflect. We begin with learning, and the first step is conferring with the teacher.

Conferring

Conferring within a minicycle is a coaching conversation that focuses on the teacher's strengths, challenges, and attributes; the conversations are highly intentional and designed to stimulate growth and change (Cheliotes & Reilly, 2018). Committed listening, paraphrasing, and reflective questioning characterize the conversation. We rotate through these three communicative actions to foster dialogue and create a space of reflection that leaves the teacher feeling affirmed and energized after the conversation. Knight (2015) refers to this as a *life-giving conversation*. The hope is that it will get the teacher excited about engaging in the coaching minicycle and spark an eagerness to discover what they may learn through the process.

The objectives of the conferring session are to

- Learn about the student's assets, proficiency levels, and learning behaviors.
- Explore instructional moves that empower language proficiency.
- Plan to implement an instructional move and determine success criteria and logistics.

The coach will go into the conferring session having already identified the first of these points: student assets, proficiency levels, and learning behaviors. Depending on the catalyst for the minicycle, the coach can start with either a discussion about the students or an exploration of instructional moves. For example, if the teacher requested the coaching minicycle because of an interest in growing the proficiency of their multilingual students, beginning with a discussion of students makes sense. However, if the cycle was initiated because the teacher wanted to explore a specific instructional move, such as implementing structured conversations or using paragraph frames to support writing instruction, then beginning with the instructional move makes more sense. In either case, the question at the forefront of the coach's mind is always this: How will multilingual students benefit from this minicycle?

Let's look at two different scenarios. Note the questions asked and how the coach and teacher identify students' assets, proficiency levels, and learning behaviors. The first scenario takes place with a 3rd grade teacher, and the focus is on multilingual student growth in general:

Coach: You mentioned you're concerned that your multilingual students don't seem engaged in class. *Tell me more about that.*

Teacher: It's really just four of my multilingual students. Gokul is a newcomer, so I understand why he doesn't say much. But Ava, Gustav, and Mikal aren't new. I just can't seem to get them to participate or share.

Coach: I noticed that Ava and Gustav were reluctant to speak with their partners when you had them turn and talk. I wondered what held them back. Their language assessment scores are both lower in speaking than in reading and writing. *What have you noticed when they do speak?*

Teacher: I vaguely remember you saying that when you shared their profile documents at the beginning of the year. Honestly, I haven't noticed much. I mean, they do speak, but not a lot. Sometimes I just think they don't know what to say.

Coach: *Which subjects are they most reluctant to engage in? Which are they more likely to engage in?*

Teacher: Gustav loves science, so he speaks up much more then. I think Ava and Mikal are more confident in math. All of them, however, are the most reluctant in writing.

Coach: You are in the fictional narratives unit now, right? I can see that trying to invent stories in a second language might make those students more reluctant.

Teacher: Yes, that's what we were pacing out when you came to planning on Monday. You know, I think you're right because when we were in the nonfiction unit, they each were much more engaged. Ava wrote her nonfiction book on Brazil. She was so proud!

Coach: I love that! It's so cool she got to share her culture with the class. So, thinking about instructional moves, *what would you want to see your students doing to show that they're engaged?*

Teacher: That's a good question. I try to have them share with a partner using a turn-and-talk before they write independently and then when they share at the end of the writing block. If they were less reluctant to talk to their partner about their writing, I think they would be more engaged, and it would help them as they work independently.

Coach: OK. I'm thinking we could try adding more structure to the turn-and-talks.

Teacher: I know I need to use sentence stems more. But if I don't plan on using them ahead of time, when I'm in the moment it feels too late. I think working with you will help me remember.

Coach: Sentence stems are a great way to add structure. I think if we pair that with thinking aloud as a linguistic scaffold, we'll see them engage more. *If this goes really well, what would Ava, Gustav, and Mikal be doing?*

Teacher: They'll look at the sentence stem and use it to share. I also hope that talking with a partner will help them understand the learning target better and get them more excited about their writing.

Our second scenario concerns a 6th grade teacher who initiated a coaching session because they wanted to learn more about using writing scaffolds with their multilingual students:

> **Teacher**: So, as I mentioned to you in my email, one of the teachers you coached, Mr. Graves, said that he worked with you on writing assignments and that it really helped his multilingual students. I want to learn more about what you did and see if I could use some new strategies with my 6th period science class. I have several students, some who are multilingual and some who are not, who could use writing support.
>
> **Coach**: We worked on scaffolding some of the writing assignments for his students. We used a couple different linguistic scaffolds. *What aspect of your students' writing do you want to see improve?*
>
> **Teacher**: All of it! But if they could use the science vocabulary correctly and more often, I would call that a win.
>
> **Coach**: Academic vocabulary and writing scaffolding go well together. Mr. Graves and I used word banks and paragraph frames as scaffolds to improve his students' writing. *What comes to mind when you hear those scaffolds?*
>
> **Teacher**: Word banks immediately make me think of a list of words students can use in their writing. I like that. What are paragraph frames?
>
> **Coach**: Paragraph frames are like fill-in-the-blank paragraphs; they help provide structure for students. We can start with a small number of blanks and then reduce them until they're just sentence starters.
>
> **Teacher**: That sounds like giving students the answers if we use that and word banks.
>
> **Coach**: It feels that way at first, but the scaffolds are temporary. *What if we differentiate based on the student's proficiency level? Which students do you feel need the most language support?*
>
> **Teacher**: All of my multilingual students are at the beginner or early intermediate level, except Patricio, who is near proficient.
>
> **Coach**: Well, we can use a word bank with the whole class and then offer paragraph frames to students who are at the beginner level, then circle back to see what we notice. *How will we know if this is successful?*

Teacher: I think if I'm using word banks in daily or weekly quick-writes and if they're using at least two or three science words in their writing, that will feel like success because right now they're using next to none.

What did you learn about the students in each scenario? How was that learning brought about? Hopefully, you noted the nature of the reflective questions (they appear italicized in the dialogue). The questions were open-ended. They were questions about the students. Open-ended questions invite longer, detailed knowledge, opinion, or feeling answers—and that's what we're after in a coaching conversation (Knight, 2015). Although this is a teacher-centered model and we're seeking to transfer instructional moves into the teacher's practice, the focus is on the students. By centering the work on the students, we create safety, and we affirm that we're not judging the teacher's capacity.

The conferring session should end with a discussion of the logistics. When will co-planning take place to ensure that the teacher embeds the instructional move into the lesson or lessons? How many coaching lessons will be planned? Is the teacher open to co-delivery? If so, what will co-delivery look like? When will a meeting take place to reflect on implementation? The answers to these questions will help determine the duration and time commitments involved in the cycle.

Co-Planning

Co-planning is the part of the cycle where we focus a bit more on teacher praxis. Here, we review the lesson, consider the instructional move selected during the conferring session, and explore how to embed it into the lesson to grow student language proficiency. In the first scenario we shared, one instructional move was to use sentence stems during turn-and-talk. In that instance, the fostering dialogue checklist discussed in Chapter 3 can help guide the co-planning conversation. (See Appendix D, Instructional Checklists.)

Using checklists to unpack all the small behaviors that make up an instructional move provides a mental model that creates clarity. As Marzano and colleagues (2020) point out, a step-by-step approach leads to expert performance. Teachers are thinking on their feet, continually doing more things than they can consciously account for. A checklist makes all that footwork visible. The coach can create a checklist based on the move selected and using language that captures the priorities of the campus.

The second scenario we looked at targeted the instructional move of scaffolding writing using paragraph frames and word banks. (See Appendix D, Instructional Checklists, for a scaffolded writing checklist.) Whether or not you choose to use a checklist as you co-plan, the objective of co-planning is to ensure the teacher is clear on what it looks like to embed the selected instructional move into the lesson. This objective can be achieved through discussion, through providing resources, or, when the teacher lacks confidence in implementing the strategy, through modeling. Modeling can involve role play, rehearsal, or modeling in real time with the class as the teacher observes.

Once the teacher understands the instructional move, it's time to discuss co-delivery. Does the teacher want you to present content while they deliver the writing strategy? Or will they introduce the science content, with you explaining the writing assignment? Or would they like you to deliver the strategy alongside them during class? Is the teacher comfortable with you supporting students who are not multilingual? Discuss these logistics beforehand to ensure a smooth delivery of the lesson.

This is also a great time to revisit the success criteria you set during conferring. If success means that students are using two to three vocabulary words in the quick-write, are there any in-class behaviors you should be on the lookout for? Will you base success solely on student work samples? This is also a great time to be open about what the reflection process can look like. Based on the flow of the conversation, you might suggest that the teacher refer to the 4-point self-rating scale shown in Figure 6.1.

Co-Delivering

This phase is the simplest to explain because we've done so much heavy lifting during conferring and co-planning. All that's left is simply to do it! In terms of the four-step empowering language proficiency process, we've completed Step 1: we've *learned* about the needs of students. We've completed Step 2: we've *planned scaffolds to implement*. Now we're at Step 3: *teach*. In this case, we're supporting teaching by coaching the teacher to provide linguistic scaffolds.

FIGURE 6.1

Scaffolded Writing Assignments Proficiency Scale

How do I self-rate in scaffolding student writing?
Rating 1–4
1: I do not provide scaffolds for writing assignments.
2: I provide scaffolds in the moment when I notice that students are having difficulty with a writing assignment.
3: I scaffold writing assignments primarily by using sentence stems.
4: I scaffold writing assignments using two or more of the following: oral rehearsal, paragraph frames, graphic organizers, sentence stems, or word banks.

Co-delivery may not be a part of every coaching minicycle. Some teachers may want to implement the strategy without an audience, whereas others will be eager to have another set of eyes and hands to see what they might miss. The decision to co-deliver must reside with the teacher; after all, it is their classroom. Preserving a level of autonomy builds trust. Ideally, you are either co-delivering the lesson or observing as the teacher delivers the lesson so you can provide coaching through reflection. In either case, you'll be taking note of how students are responding to the instructional move, as well as any other relevant observations (Dove & Honigsfeld, 2017). Putting on a reflective hat while co-delivering will provide insight when it's time to reflect on implementation.

Reflecting

Instructional improvement hinges on the reflection that takes place after lesson delivery. In addition to using committed listening, paraphrasing, and reflective questioning, the coach adds feedback as an essential part of the conversation. From a coaching stance, feedback is the information loop between the coach and the coachee that raises awareness of how their instructional moves affect student learning. As learners, knowing where we stand in relation to a target helps us determine how to move forward.

Not all feedback is created equal; it can take many forms and structures. We're after *reflective feedback* (Kee et al., 2010). Reflective feedback energizes, clarifies, and provokes thought or action. Our conversation partner walks away excited to continue implementing an instructional strategy, either understanding the strategy at a deeper level or thinking about how to implement it differently.

Monitoring our own and our partner's emotions then using that information as a guide promotes productive conversations. Are we entering the conversation believing change is possible? Believing the best about our conversation partner? Mindset is everything when it comes to creating change. As author Peter Senge (Strategies for Influence, n.d.) wrote, "You cannot force commitment.... You nudge a little here, inspire a little there, and provide a role model. Your primary influence is the environment you create." Each coaching conversation is an opportunity to nudge and inspire. Our aim is to influence change by creating an environment where reflection can flourish.

With reflective feedback comes reflective questioning, and the combination of these two forms of communication comprises the final phase of the coaching minicycle. Here, we partner with teachers to process and unpack the effect of the instructional move on students. In terms of the four-step empowering language proficiency process, we're in Step 4: *reflect*.

The following questions are great starting points for the coaching conversation:

- What did you notice about how students responded to the move?
- What surprised you?
- What confirmed something you already knew?
- What effect did the move have on student participation? On student work products? On understanding?
- How would you rate your/our implementation of the move? Why?
- What specific actions made the instructional move effective?
- What specific actions could enhance its effect on students?

As teachers respond to these questions, the coach practices committed listening, followed by paraphrasing. Paraphrasing can clarify, summarize, or shift thinking (Kee et al., 2010). Let's look at the importance of paraphrasing in the context of scenario two. The coach has asked the teacher to reflect on the effect of using writing scaffolds with their multilingual students:

Coach: *What did you notice about how students responded to the scaffolded writing assignment?*

Teacher: I noticed that, in general, student responses include more academic vocabulary. Several students used all the words provided in the bank, including Patricio. My early intermediate students like Jaime, Erik, and Peng used a lot more of the words, and the paragraph frames were a game-changer for my beginners. I was worried that it would be like giving them the answers, but as they wrote, I saw how focused they were, and their responses showed it too.

Coach: *And what else?*

Teacher: Now I'm wondering if I should adjust the frames and give them to the early intermediate students, although I don't want any of them to become dependent on the frames.

The coach can respond in one of three ways:

Coach clarifies: So, you're juggling two concerns, and both have pros and cons: students not producing quality writing or becoming overly dependent on scaffolds.

Coach summarizes: The optimism in your voice is exciting! Trying something new can be daunting, but it sounds like your risk taking is paying off for your students.

Coach shifts thinking: The high expectations you have for our multilingual students is so important. You're balancing scaffolding for language with challenging them. That's such a huge part of having an asset-based mindset.

In each of these closing comments, the coach uses value statements to paraphrase. Value statements are an important part of operating in nonjudgment and generosity, two important elements of trust. Nonjudgment means that both conversation partners can ask for what they need without judgment; generosity means we extend the most generous interpretation possible to the intentions, words, and actions of others (Brown, 2018). Paraphrasing using value statements demonstrates that we believe in the teacher's ability to grow their instructional practice and are actively committed to looking for and naming that growth. A paraphrase is best followed by a pause to enable our thinking partner time to process what we've said. We believe in the power of wait time as it pertains to student learning, but we often forget the power it can have in our communications with adults.

Asking, "And what else?" (Knight, 2017) is another way to nudge teachers toward saying more as we say less. The hallmark of a successful coaching conversation is the teacher doing most of the talking. Elena Aguilar (2013) describes the effect of quiet listening this way: "It demonstrates respect when we listen to someone from this space, believing they will come to their own understanding, and that my own understanding is not necessarily better than theirs" (p. 150). Who *wouldn't* want to be a part of a conversation like that? These are life-giving conversations.

After reflective questioning and feedback, as well as paraphrasing with value statements, it's time to determine next steps. Perhaps the teacher feels they can carry forward with what they've learned, and now they want to move to informal check-ins. Or maybe this experience has piqued the teacher's curiosity; maybe they would like to co-plan another scaffolded writing assignment, see you model a lesson, or have you observe them and provide more feedback.

It's important to ensure there will be some form of follow-up, be it formal or informal. Closing the reflective phase with questions like the ones listed here will enable us to keep our eye on continuous improvement:

- How would you like me to check in on student progress moving forward?
- How will you know when this move has become an organic part of your teaching tool box?
- What would you like me to follow up with you?
- What do you need from me to maintain student progress?
- If we partnered together again, what would you want to change? What would you want to keep the same?

Implementing: Questions to Consider

Coaching is all about creating a collaborative partnership to build teacher capacity through conversations that are life-giving and centered on student learning. The majority of the heavy lifting within this coaching model takes place during coaching conversations. In fact, the cycle begins and ends with coaching conversations.

What about this model do you find compelling? In what ways will this model move forward campus goals, student achievement, and your own personal coaching and leadership abilities? What might prevent this model from being successful? How can you tweak this model to overcome these roadblocks? Are the potential benefits worth the effort? Why or why not? Examining the model from multiple vantage points can increase the effectiveness of implementation.

The Co-Teaching Cycle

Co-teaching cycles are the deepest level of partnership we can engage in as we coach teachers for the success of multilingual learners. When we co-teach, we're embedding ourselves fully with the content teacher and their class. Because of the highly collaborative nature of this teacher-centered model, coaches or those in specialist roles are best suited to implement these cycles. Co-teaching cycles are professional learning opportunities that enable the content teacher and the coach to cultivate their beliefs, their pedagogical knowledge and skills, and their areas of growth (Dove & Honigsfeld, 2017).

These cycles have the most potential to contribute to teacher praxis and transfer of skills. When a coach plans, teaches, and reflects alongside a teacher several times a week, organic reflective dialogue happens, and a level of metacognition transpires that neither party would experience apart from this form of professional learning. The depth of partnership, as well as its length and duration, are intended to promote measurable student growth and sustainability for content teachers.

At the close of the cycle, we want to consider the following questions, so it's prudent to begin with the end in mind:

- How have students grown as a result of the cycle?
- What evidence supports this?
- How have the teacher's pedagogy and instructional beliefs shifted as a result of the cycle?
- Have these shifts become autonomous behaviors that the teacher uses easily, fluently, and with adaptability? (Marzano et al., 2020)

Logistically, cycles may range from 4 to 12 weeks, depending on the frequency of co-delivery, the goal set for the students or teacher, and the availability of the coach facilitating the cycle. The shorter the cycle, the more consecutive days a coach should be co-delivering instruction. If a cycle is scheduled to last four weeks, then co-delivering instruction should take place a minimum of three days each week to yield the best results. If a cycle is scheduled to last 12 weeks, then co-teaching two lessons each week can lead to goal attainment.

Setting a SMART goal is essential in this coaching model because it drives each phase of the cycle. Without clearly stated goals, success indicators can become nebulous, leaving the coach wondering, "What have I accomplished?" The goals set can pertain to the student, the teacher, or both.

My first co-teaching cycle was with a 1st grade teacher who was brand new to the district; she had three multilingual students new to U.S. schools. My principal asked me to immediately start working with her and her students. I was elated. I had already attended several days of training offered by my department to teach me about my new role as language coach and about the new model of serving multilingual learners. I had spent the summer reading, researching, and wondering, and now it was time to put all that reading and research into action. It was time to coach! I was ready—or so I thought.

During our first week of campus professional development, I made sure to introduce myself to the teacher, Dana, reciting my love of 1st grade and my excitement to work with her and the newcomers in her class. As luck would have it, Dana was thrilled to know I would be working with her students. "So, how does this work?" she asked curiously. Here's how I responded:

> I'm new to campus, too, so we'll learn together. I'll do a mixture of pulling the girls out for small-group lessons and supporting you in class the first few weeks. Once you're settled with your class, I'll come in a few days each week and work with the girls during a content block to support you in any way I can. I'll also join your team planning meetings, and we can work forward from there.

Dana nodded, then shrugged noncommittally. "That's different, but I think I might like it," she said. I smiled and shifted to asking about her summer; it was time to make connections and build trust. It turns out that Dana did, in fact, love having me in class. I spent *the entire semester* working with her and her students during the literacy block three days each week.

I'm not sure I maximized the amount of transfer of linguistically scaffolded instructional moves, but I did learn a valuable lesson. To measure impact, coaching in general and co-teaching cycles in particular must have clearly defined boundaries. I spent lots of time in class with Dana and our students, but something wasn't clicking. Eight weeks into this "support," I wasn't sure if I was successful.

What *was* success? Dana loved having me in class supporting her and the students. We planned and led small reading and writing groups and co-taught the reading minilessons. Was that success? As a former 1st grade teacher and literacy enthusiast, I loved working with her and the students, especially seeing the growth of our newcomers. But did my enjoyment translate into results? By the way, exactly what results were I looking for?

Since that time, I've learned that goals are vital to measuring the impact of coaching work. Diane Sweeney and Leanne Harris (2020) summarize this idea well: "It is no longer okay to judge our success simply on whether or not teachers like us or find us to be helpful" (p. 47). We need clear data, both quantitative and qualitative, to let us know the effect we're having on student and teacher learning. Dana and I enjoyed working together, and she often mentioned how much easier I made teaching. I often thanked her for being so warm and welcoming and for allowing me to learn how to be a coach with her. The experience felt good, and I used my mistakes as opportunities to grow. However, I now know that all those warm feelings aside, building teacher capacity and growing student learning and language proficiency are central to my work as a coach for multilingual learners. As Maya Angelou put it, now that I know better, I can do better.

Before You Begin

The decision to enter into a co-teaching cycle with a teacher is made based on data and the needs of multilingual students. Co-teaching cycles can grow out of Inclusion with a Purpose or Coaching Minicycles. A classroom with a significant number of multilingual learners is ideal for co-teaching cycles. A "significant number" is relative, of course. If all classes have multilingual learners, then it's important to consider the level of language proficiency and the progress students are making academically and toward reclassification.

Preparation for a co-teaching cycle mirrors that for a coaching minicycle. Observing students in class, analyzing data, and attending collaborative planning are all steps you should take before initiating a co-teaching cycle with a teacher. The key difference between the two preparations is in mindset. The focus of a coaching minicycle is embedding one specific instructional move into lesson delivery that will grow the language proficiency of multilingual students. In contrast, in a co-teaching cycle, the coach fully partners with the content teacher to implement various linguistic scaffolds, instructional moves, and strategies to reach a specific learning goal for students or a specific teaching goal for the teacher. Here, our mindset is more panoramic. We're reviewing multiple data points and observing from various vantage points, asking ourselves

- What are the language needs of the students in the class?
- What specific linguistic scaffolds and instructional moves will grow students' language proficiency?
- What linguistic scaffolds are currently in place?
- How are students responding to them?
- What instructional moves will enhance their effectiveness?

After observing and analyzing data, be sure to synthesize the information and formulate considerations, entry points, and recommendations. This is the science of coaching. Artistry comes into play when we confer with teachers, which is the next step before launching the co-teaching cycle.

Conferring

Conferring before beginning a co-teaching cycle is similar to the conversation we have before engaging in a coaching minicycle. Committed listening, paraphrasing, and reflective questions are staples in these dialogues. However, the co-teaching conferring session differs in depth and precision. Let's look at Step 1 of the empowering language proficiency process: learn. With the co-teaching model, we unpack student language data and learning behaviors more closely in view of setting a SMART goal. The objectives of the conferring session are to

- Learn and discuss the assets, proficiency levels, and learning behaviors of students.
- Consider the effectiveness of current linguistic scaffolds.
- Determine student and teacher goals, and set success criteria.
- Discuss partnership preferences, and establish norms and logistics.

Ideally, classroom teachers are all participating in the "learn" step of the growing language proficiency process. At the beginning of the year, instructional leaders or a language coach should be providing linguistic data about multilingual students so teachers can prepare to meet their language needs. Reviewing linguistic or academic data and delivering small- or whole-group instruction provide opportunities to learn about the proficiency levels, assets, and learning behaviors and styles of multilingual learners.

In my home state of Texas, we're required to select and document which linguistic accommodations multilingual learners are receiving. (Once scaffolds are documented, they're considered accommodations.) In my first year as a language coach, I viewed this legal task merely as a formality. Teachers would often choose every scaffold. In the course of professional learning and coaching conversations, however, we began to use the document that listed the student linguistic accommodations as a tool to reflect on the instruction that multilingual students received. Meeting with teachers to discuss the specific language needs and academic performance of multilingual students became a rhythm. Taking time to guide teachers in narrowing down the proficiency-based scaffolds to three to five only then monitoring and adjusting the scaffolds throughout the year increased teacher learning around language acquisition.

The conferring questions listed in Figure 6.2 can provide a starting point for the coaching conversation.

Again, this is where the artistry emerges. The entry point of the conversation will vary, based on the relationship with the teacher, the catalyst for interest in the co-teaching cycle, and, most important, the needs of the students. Reflective questioning, committed listening, and paraphrasing should guide the conversation toward a goal. The student goal should target the needs of most of the multilingual students in the class. The teacher may choose to set a goal for themselves during this time, or that goal may emerge during the cycle.

FIGURE 6.2

Conferring Questions: Co-Teaching Cycle

Teaching Multilingual Students	Unpacking the Needs of Multilingual Students	Establishing Goals
• How are your multilingual students performing? • What has been most rewarding, surprising, or challenging with your multilingual students? • What are your favorite strategies to use when teaching multilingual students? • What do you know about/have experienced with co-teaching? • Have you noticed anything unique about your multilingual students that is key to serving them well? • What cultural assets and prior knowledge have you noticed? How can we build on those?	• What linguistic scaffolds do you use most often with each multilingual student? • How are students responding to the linguistic scaffolds used in class? • Which domain do your multilingual students, both in general and individually, show strength in? In which domain would you like to see growth? • In what ways are your students independent learners? • In what ways are your students dependent learners?	• How would you like your multilingual students to grow as a result of this co-teaching cycle? • If this cycle is successful, how would you know? • What do you want for yourself or your students once this cycle ends? • What is one specific skill you would like to see your students develop? Why? • What would indicate they have developed this skill? • If they develop this skill, how would it affect them as learners?

Let's now consider a third scenario that shows what a conferring conversation for a co-teaching cycle might sound like. This one focuses on academic vocabulary and takes place in the context of 4th grade math:

Coach: *What has been most surprising, rewarding, or challenging with your multilingual students so far this year?*

Teacher: Seeing Amir's growth from the first day until now has been really rewarding. The first few weeks he was so quiet, and I could tell he was nervous. Now he's much more comfortable. He has started speaking with his table group occasionally.

Coach: That's exciting to see! He came out of his silent period faster than I expected. I can tell you've been intentional about making him feel comfortable. Your classroom is really inviting. *How do you feel about your multilingual students' performance in general?*

Teacher: Overall, just OK. I wanted to do this co-teaching cycle because the coaching minicycle on structured conversations really made a difference for all my kids. It challenged me to put more visuals and sentence stems in my lessons. The kids were talking more, and the lessons just felt better. I want to do more of that.

Coach: I'm so glad you found that the structured conversations made a difference. I'm excited to continue working together. When I looked over the data, I saw that a lot of your multilingual students are at the near-proficient level, pretty close to reclassification. Structured conversations could really help them toward reclassifying. *What have you noticed about their speaking abilities?* I brought a list of observable behaviors for the near-proficient level in the speaking domain. You can glance at those and see if any behaviors match what you see in class.

Teacher: I think most of my multilingual students are able to have extended conversations. I haven't noticed language errors when they speak, but I do think content-specific vocabulary is an area they could use support with. They seem like native speakers most of the time. Kira, Saanvi, Evan, and Marco would all reclassify if it were up to me! Of course, Amir needs more time, and I do notice a few things with Jian and Katya, mostly in their writing.

Coach: Content-specific vocabulary would be a great area to target, especially if we want to work toward reclassifying those four. *As far as Jian and Katya are concerned, what have you noticed with them?*

Teacher: The descriptors mentioned second language errors. Jian used the word "teached" in his math journal recently; that stood out to me. Overall, I think vocabulary will benefit all my multilingual students and even those who aren't multilingual.

Coach: So, at the end of our co-teaching cycle, *what difference would you want to see in their vocabulary?*

Teacher: I'd like to see students use more academic vocabulary when they're explaining their thinking. Math comes to mind right now because that's the subject we focused on for structured conversations.

Coach: OK. I'm thinking we could measure that with their responses during structured conversations, when they write in their journal, and on independent work assignments where they have to explain their thinking. I want it to be a specific goal we can measure.

Teacher: So maybe we'll want them to use three academic vocabulary words each time they explain their thinking?

Coach: Exactly! I think you just found our goal. We can break down the steps when we actually co-plan the lessons. Which days do you want me to plan to be in class with you?

Let's look again at the questions the coach asked:

- What has been most surprising, rewarding, or challenging with your multilingual students so far this year?
- How do you feel about your multilingual students' performance in general?
- What have you noticed about their speaking abilities?
- What have you noticed with Jian and Katya?
- What difference would you want to see in their vocabulary?

Please note that these questions all *center on the students*.

We also see the importance of preparation here. The coach was able to navigate the conversation toward student performance by having looked at the data beforehand and by bringing a resource that listed observable behaviors to build the teacher's awareness and capacity to notice and name specific language behaviors. The final element of the conferring conversation focuses on logistics, such as which days the coach will join in teaching, how long the cycle might last, and when co-planning meetings will take place.

Co-Planning

A successful co-teaching cycle is contingent on successful co-planning. During a co-teaching cycle, a coach should be attending the regular or weekly team or department planning sessions with the content teacher and their larger team. This ensures that the coach has full context for instruction. It also ensures that the co-planning meeting that takes place between the coach and the content teacher—this is separate from the larger planning—is more efficient because there's a solid starting place. Although teams and departments plan together, each teacher has to customize those plans to meet the needs of their students.

Co-planning will likely happen once a week for each week of the cycle. The first co-planning session is the most important because it will establish the norms of the partnership. Taking time to discuss preferences, roles, and such issues as classroom management will set the tone. Does the teacher want to introduce you to the class, or do they want you to just blend in seamlessly? Are there things you should know about the students in class who are not multilingual? Is the teacher comfortable with you redirecting students? If so, in what way? Considering questions like these is best done early on.

You should accomplish three things during each co-planning session. You should

1. Review the lesson sequence and assess language demands.
2. Embed moves into lessons. These can include linguistic scaffolds, language-rich instructional moves, and engagement strategies.
3. Determine your roles in co-delivery.

Language demands describe the linguistic expectations inherent within the learning tasks you've assigned to students. What will students need to do during lesson delivery to understand the content? What behaviors will they exhibit to demonstrate they're gaining content knowledge (Fenner & Snyder 2017)? Next, you'll need to *embed moves* into the lesson to help students meet those demands. What scaffolds will support students in using the language to ensure they understand the content? What language-rich instructional moves will make the content accessible to students at various proficiency levels? What engagement strategies will ensure that students' affective filters are low so they can learn? The list of questions shared in Appendix E, Coaching Questions for Linguistic Growth, can provide more specific considerations during these one-on-one co-planning sessions.

Determining roles in co-delivery is the final discussion point in co-planning. The coach may be better suited to lead a segment of the lesson that involves a new engagement strategy they suggested, whereas the content teacher would be better positioned to explain a key mathematical concept. Discussing roles during co-planning ensures a smooth co-delivery of the lesson.

Figure 6.3 shows a sample lesson plan for another scenario, which focuses on using academic vocabulary in the context of 4th grade math. The figure lists the lesson on the left, with documentation concerning the language demands and scaffolds

FIGURE 6.3
Lesson Sample with Scaffolds (4th Grade): Introducing Multistep Multiplication Problems

Co-teaching cycle goal: At the end of an 8-week cycle, students will explain their mathematical thinking using three academic vocabulary words in at least six of eight responses.

Today's lesson objective: Students will analyze the process of solving multistep multiplication problems by sorting and sequencing the steps needed to correctly solve the problem.

I can statement: I can identify and sort the steps to solving a multistep multiplication problem.

Engage	Language Demands
Ask: Have you ever used a recipe to help someone make a meal? **New Learning** Today we're going to learn that when mathematicians solve multistep word problems, they follow steps just like a chef does when they make a new dish. 1. Read the word problem, as well as the steps listed on the sentence strips. (Make sure the steps are all mixed up.) 2. Model placing the steps in the correct order to solve the problem. **Guided Practice** 1. Read the practice problem to students. 2. Put students in pairs, and have them work together to place the steps in the correct order. 3. Bring the class back together to review and explain the correct order of steps. **Independent Practice** Students will receive two practice problems. They will cut out, sort, and glue the steps in the correct order in their math journals.	What will students need to do during lesson delivery to understand the content? What behaviors will they exhibit to demonstrate they're gaining content knowledge? Students will need to • Know the word *recipe*. • Use sequence words (*first, next, last*). • Read the word problems. • Listen and share ideas with a partner. **Language Scaffolds** What scaffolds will support students in using the language so they can understand the content? What language-rich instructional moves will make the content accessible to students at various proficiency levels? What engagement strategies will ensure students' affective filters are low so they can learn? Teachers will need to • Show a visual or recipe or use realia. • Use QSSSA to have a structured conversation in which students share a time they used a recipe. • Check the sample word problem for unfamiliar vocabulary or words with multiple meanings. • Generate sentence stems to match how a mathematician would think aloud when sequencing the problems and use these stems when modeling how to place the steps in order. • Make sure sentence stems are posted for all to see as students work in pairs.

Math Stations

Content teacher: Small group: review multiplication problems
Coach: Small group: explain mathematical thinking with one-step multiplication problems

shown on the right. By unpacking the language demands and selecting language scaffolds, instruction becomes more linguistically accommodated and more focused on increasing students' language proficiency.

Co-Delivering

In Co-Teaching for English Learners, Dove and Honigsfeld (2017) outline seven different co-teaching formats. These formats are distinguished by student groupings; either both teachers teach the students as a whole group or they teach two separate groups, focusing on the same or different content based on student needs. In the lesson shown in Figure 6.3, both teachers can begin by team-teaching the lesson, then transition into small-group teaching once students begin their math stations. The instructional frameworks used on your campus will help you determine co-delivery formats and roles. Certain subjects may lend themselves to team teaching, whereas others may more naturally align with a focus on working with small groups.

During co-delivery, the coach should engage in "reflection in action" (Dove & Honigsfeld, 2017), taking note of student responses to the language scaffolds. Are the scaffolds increasing students' ability to access, engage with, and understand content? Are the scaffolds limiting the students from demonstrating understanding? Taking note of these things will support the reflection phase that comes after co-delivery and that flows back into co-planning the next lesson in the unit.

Reflecting

At the beginning of your next co-planning meeting, it makes sense to begin with reflection on co-delivery, primarily taking time to evaluate the students' responses to the lesson.

The coach has shared linguistic and language-rich strategies for the teacher to use. Now it's time to determine whether pushing the teacher toward setting a goal will enhance the overall co-teaching cycle.

Adult learners require autonomy. This principle of *andragogy,* a term coined by American educator Malcolm Knowles, is known as *self-concept* (Lee, 2024). It means that adults need to feel responsible for their learning; they prefer self-direction, making their own decisions, and managing their own learning (Instructional Design

Australia, 2024). When considering how to encourage a teacher to set a goal, Elena Aguilar (2020) describes gaps in learning not as deficits but as areas of growth that include skill, knowledge, capacity, will, cultural competence, and emotional intelligence.

Most professional learning, including coaching, centers around skill and knowledge gaps. These are often the safer and easier gaps to address. Addressing the capacity and will gaps requires more energy and emotional agility because both are both greatly affected by school culture, climate, and leadership. The last two areas noted—cultural competency and emotional intelligence—are often the most neglected, but they're crucial in our work with multilingual students.

When coaches ask teachers to set goals, the teachers must have the psychological safety to do so. John C. Maxwell (2011) shares an important leadership principle: Don't pretend you're perfect. Be open to admitting faults, asking for advice, and learning from others. As coaches, we must not show up as an expert but as a partner. Our goal isn't to fix the teacher or the instruction. Instead, it's to come alongside and grow multilingual students' language proficiency by offering more brain power and hands than the teacher has alone.

Our hope is that the entire co-teaching cycle serves as a safe professional learning opportunity, that we have created a safe space of reflection that invigorates teachers and positively affects student learning. Figure 6.4 includes four reflective conversation structures, as well as a set of general reflection questions that coaches can use during this phase. Conversation structures like these promote thoughtful—and safe—reflection.

Implementing: Questions to Consider

It's now time to consider implementation. What about this model is compelling? In what ways could you adapt it to fit the needs of your campus or district? Do particular students come to mind as you consider this model? What might prevent implementation? Does your existing climate, culture, and instructional frameworks support this model? How could growth toward this type of professional learning occur?

Co-teaching is the most collaborative and intense of all the coaching models. Before implementing this cycle, it's beneficial to compare the time investment with the potential outcome. What outcomes do you desire? Can you commit to implementing each phase of the cycle? Reflecting on these ideas independently and with a leadership team can be key to determining next steps.

FIGURE 6.4

Reflective Conversation Structures

Reflective Conversation Structures	Reflection Questions
Notice and Wonder (Dove & Honigsfeld, 2017) Let's share something we noticed during our lesson and something we're still wondering about. Do you want to share first, or would you like me to?	• What went well in our lesson? • What could we have done differently? • Which students do you feel really understood the content? • Which students may need to be retaught? • What do we notice about student work? • Were students engaged during the lesson? How do we know?
2 by 2 Let's share two things we loved and two things we would adjust if we repeated that lesson or would consider moving forward.	
Glow and Grow Let's share one thing we really felt glowed about our lesson and one thing we think we can tweak to grow our students.	
Self-Rate Are you interested in using or creating a proficiency scale to measure your growth in delivering parts of the lesson? On a scale of 1 to 10, how would you rate our lesson? Why? (Knight, 2018)	

Prerequisites to Consider

We have now explored all five coaching models. Let's take a moment to consider the prerequisites needed to launch this type of professional learning. A first necessity is *a culture of collaboration*. A campus that strives to operate as a professional learning community defined by collaboration and continuous improvement is conducive to the coaching models we've unpacked. Such campuses have an ecosystem of professional learning that embeds coaching into school improvement so learning is aligned, connected, and meaningful for students and teachers (Sweeney & Harris, 2020). Instructional leaders model being the lead learner and by doing so, normalize continuous improvement. Administrators build and maintain trust by being strategic and intentional with the initiatives they select and monitor. This avoids initiative fatigue and the chronic educational problem of doing too many things at merely a surface level.

In this sort of climate, educators buy into initiatives more easily because they trust in the thoughtful and focused leadership of their administrators. In turn, teachers feel safe to engage in professional learning and coaching. They're energized by the experiences because they know how relevant and meaningful they are—and because they can put them to use right away. The coaching models we've explored provide opportunities for coaches and instructional leaders to share resources, strategies, and experiences that are immediately applicable and add value to student learning.

A second necessity is *an asset-based approach to coaching*. Our aim is to grow the language proficiency of multilingual students toward reclassifying as English proficient, and asset-based beliefs and equity-driven practices are foundational to this goal. Our schools must be places where culturally and linguistically diverse students can thrive. They must be welcoming and inclusive environments committed to affirming the personhood of all learners. They must empower students to become independent learners through high expectations and the provision of appropriate language and learning scaffolds. Conditions like these will lead to equitable outcomes for multilingual learners.

If, however, these necessary prerequisites are missing from your current reality, it is important to consider what steps you, as an instructional leader, can take to begin cultivating these prerequisites. How can you encourage a culture of collaboration? What might it look like to model an asset-based mindset toward both coaching and multilingual students? Rather than accepting a climate that isn't conducive to the success of multilingual students, let's be the change agent our students need.

Tying It Up

In this chapter, we have investigated how to put our theory into practice through teacher-centered coaching models. These models target student learning by working directly with teachers to embed linguistic scaffolds and instructional moves into instruction that grows language proficiency. Coaching conversations drive these models by using communication as a vehicle to partner with teachers for professional learning. Partnership and communication are two of our core coaching beliefs that comprise the "moves" or hands of our coaching practice. These teacher-centered coaching models create spaces of reflection and opportunities for praxis that lead to transfer. The desired outcome is that students and teachers are more self-sufficient in their use of language and language scaffolds. The coach or instructional leader measures success by the self-sufficiency they leave behind once the cycles of professional learning have come to a close.

Mind Your Ms

Maximize Your Motivation

- Reflect on a coaching conversation you've had with a teacher, colleague, or friend. Write down what you remember them sharing. Next, write three paraphrases: one to clarify, one to summarize, and one to shift thinking.
- Select one of the reflective conversation structures we've discussed—for example, notice and wonder, 2 by 2, or glow and grow (see Figure 6.4). After conversing with a colleague, delivering professional learning, or working with a student, journal to practice giving yourself reflective feedback.

Mold Your Mindset

- In writing, compare the two teacher-centered models of Coaching Minicycles and Co-Teaching cycles.
- Research and read about teacher-centered coaching models to grow your skill set. Here are some suggestions:
  - *Co-Teaching for English Learners: A Guide to Collaborative Planning, Instruction, Assessment, and Reflection* (2017), by Maria Dove and Andrea Honigsfeld

- *The Essential Guide for Student-Centered Coaching: What Every K–12 Coach and School Leader Needs to Know* (2020), by Diane Sweeney and Leanna S. Harris
- *Coaching Conversations: Transforming Your School One Conversation at a Time* (2018), by Linda M. Gross Cheliotes and Marceta F. Reilly

Make Your Moves
- Review Figure 6.2: Conferring Questions: Co-Teaching Cycle. Reword the questions using your own unique coaching voice.
- Review the conversations between the coach and teacher in each of the three scenarios described in this chapter. What do you notice about the coach's moves? What would you change? How might those conversations sound with a teacher in your sphere of influence?

Conclusion

Enjoy the Journey

The destination is the journey itself. My time as an educator and a coach has made this idea come alive. However, people often buy into a philosophical sentiment called *the arrival fallacy*. The term, introduced by positive psychologist Tal Ben-Shahar, refers to the illusion that joy lies at the destination ahead (Khalifeh, 2023). It might sound like, "Once I become a coach, *then* I'll feel accomplished," or, "Once student language scores go up, *then* my administrators will see my value as a leader." Feeling accomplished or valued as a leader is understandable. But staking our happiness or even our self-worth on factors outside our control is dangerous. Ghada Khalifeh (2023) shares a powerful quote from Tal Ben-Shahar in her article "How High Achievers Can Avoid the Arrival Fallacy":

> Attaining lasting happiness requires that we enjoy the journey on our way toward a destination we deem valuable. Happiness is not about making it to the peak of the mountain nor is it about climbing aimlessly around the mountain; happiness is the experience of climbing toward the peak. (para. 14)

The first time I encountered her article, I read those lines several times. "Enjoy the journey." "Happiness is the experience of climbing toward the peak." These words jumped off the screen toward me.

Having entered the field of coaching and become a coach of coaches, I've had the opportunity to spend lots of time reflecting. My most important reflection is to be present in the moment by realizing that the destination is the journey itself. Do I have goals? Milestones I want to accomplish? Absolutely, but I can best achieve happiness by enjoying the steps along the way.

Embrace Change

Our journey through coaching for multilingual students' success has explored motivations, mindsets, and moves that can build the capacity of all stakeholders to serve multilingual students. As our world becomes smaller through technology, we become global citizens who are more aware of the people, cultures, and worlds outside our own. Our classrooms are more diverse and, as a result, must be more inclusive than ever. Inclusivity doesn't happen by chance; it happens through intentionality.

As our journey together comes to a close, I invite you to consider where *you* are in your own coaching and leadership journey for the success of multilingual students. What is your current reality? What changes would you like to make in your own practice? Why? It's unlikely that you'll take all the ideas in this book and apply them all at once. Go slow to go fast. The best place for a coach or leader to start is within. Develop your own coaching or leadership manifesto. Before we can coach or lead others, we have to coach and lead ourselves. Take your time; tiny tweaks add up to great gains. Lasting change happens when we're clear on our motives for change, have spent time in reflection to adjust our mindset, and calculate which moves will yield the results we desire.

So, as you reflect on all we have learned on this journey, take time to consider where you might land on the stages of change (see Figure C.1). Be transparent about where you are at the moment. Be thoughtful about where you would like to go. Most important, be compassionate with yourself about how you'll get there. As the famous proverb says, a journey of a thousand miles begins with a single step.

FIGURE C.1
Stages of Change

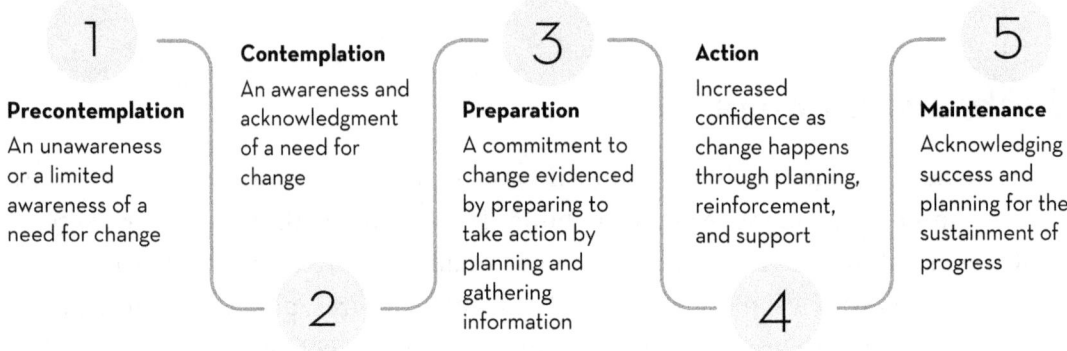

Source: Adapted from DiClemente and Prochaska's Six Stages of Change, 1983.

Acknowledgments

Writing a published book has been a dream of mine as an avid reader and lover of books and learning. Taking this writing journey has been a rewarding and challenging experience. It is true when people say it feels impossible until it's done; I now fully understand! Taking time to show gratitude to those who have coached and empowered me along the way is an honor.

I would like to begin by thanking the colleagues who have collaborated and influenced me on my educational leadership journey. To "The Power Team," Aimee, Laurea, Lisa, and Jordan, working with you has been one of the best professional experiences I've had thus far. Much of what is written in these pages has been influenced by the great work our team accomplished together. Aimee, your futuristic and compassionate leadership created an environment for others to learn, lead, and shine. Laurea, your empowering leadership cultivated an atmosphere of constant growth. Lisa, your calm and steady leadership provides an authentic space for others to show up as themselves, be appreciated, and thrive. Jordan, your diligence and commitment to excellence makes others better.

To the principals who trusted me to step into instructional leadership as a coach, I am grateful. Susie, your objective, diligent style of leading allowed me to grow as a leader. Thanks for suggesting I apply as an LC; it truly set me on a great path. Phyllis, thank you for trusting me to lead from day one. Your confidence in me allowed me to shine in my department and open doors. I am because you are; thank you.

Thank you to the editors at ASCD. Susan, from proposal to manuscript and throughout development, you were extremely helpful. Your check-ins and feedback kept me on track. Megan, I appreciate your clear communication and for taking my considerations to heart.

To my family, I am so very grateful. Andre, thank you for being a true and supportive partner. I appreciate how you take time to show you care, especially by reading through snippets of educational jargon! Your encouragement in all my endeavors is invaluable. Preston and Peyton, thank you for shaping and growing me as a human; guiding you has been one of my greatest lessons. I am grateful for the many times you checked in on me as I wrote, bringing me snacks and reminding me to take breaks. To my mom for sparking my love of reading with trips to the library and money for scholastic book fairs! Your pride spurs me onward. Keiondra, thank you for reading my first proposal and all the random paragraphs and edits at odd times. Aunt Madeline, thank you for always asking for an update and reminding me I am an author even before it's released. To all friends and coworkers who inquired about the book, thank you for sharing the enthusiasm of this milestone. You are appreciated.

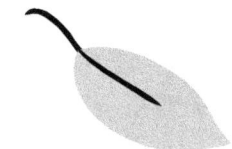

Appendixes

Appendix A	Self-Rating Tools A–C
Appendix B	Terms for Students and Programs
Appendix C	Instructional Routines for Structured Conversations
Appendix D	Instructional Checklists
Appendix E	Coaching Questions for Linguistic Growth

Appendix A

Self-Rating Tools A–C

Tool A: Committed Listening

When we listen with commitment, we convey "I care about what you have to say, and I'm listening with all my senses so I fully understand the issue from your perspective" (Kee et al., 2010, p. 95).

Scale	Proficiency Level	Descriptor
1	Aspiring	I demonstrate listening by giving advice, offering opinions, and making personal connections as my conversation partner shares their thoughts. I often share my thoughts equally.
2	Dawning	I demonstrate listening through nonverbal attention such as facial expressions, gestures, and posture often interjected with comments or questions that redirect the conversation or the speaker's train of thought.
3	Learning	I demonstrate committed listening by limiting my own connections and questions to attend more fully to the speaker, sometimes providing compliments and comments that guide the conversation.
4	Reflecting	I set aside judgment, advice, and personal connections to demonstrate committed listening by • Ensuring there are no distractions so I may fully attend to the speaker. • Asking questions that provide clarity and do not interrupt their train of thought or redirect the conversation. • Pause to consider the speaker's words so that I can provide a thoughtful response that centers the speaker.

Notes:

Tool B: Paraphrasing

"Paraphrasing is intended to align the people in a conversation and create a safe environment for thinking" (Kee et al., 2010, p. 107).

Scale	Proficiency Level	Descriptor
1	Aspiring	I listen while the speaker is talking and ask questions or pose comments rather than paraphrase their thoughts.
2	Dawning	I parrot the speaker's words back to them before I ask questions and comment with my thoughts or opinions.
3	Learning	I quickly parrot the speaker's words using "you" statements to center the speaker before I ask questions that clarify or guide the conversation in a way that helps me.
4	Reflecting	I first pause then paraphrase the speaker's words in my own using "you" statements, and then I probe to ensure the message I heard matches the speaker's intentions (i.e., the three Ps: pause, paraphrase, probe).

Notes:

Tool C: *Powerful Questioning*

"The powerful question serves as a key to unlock the chamber that was holding our thoughts captive" (Kee et al., 2010, p. 127).

Scale	Proficiency Level	Descriptor
1	Aspiring	I make statements posed as questions that may elicit defensive or reactive responses. *You don't use the linguistic accommodations you chose for the student, do you?*
2	Dawning	I ask close-ended and sometimes right-or-wrong questions I may know the answer to in order to stump or call out my conversation partner. *Are you actually using any of the linguistic accommodations you chose for the student?*
3	Learning	I ask opinion questions that elicit short or hesitant responses in order to elicit a response that primarily serves my purposes. *Do you feel that the linguistic accommodations are beneficial?*
4	Reflecting	I ask open-ended or opinion questions that presume positive intent and elicit longer detailed responses that cause my conversation to reflect on their thoughts, position, or actions. *Which linguistic accommodations work best for this student?*

Notes:

Appendix B

Terms for Students and Programs

	Terms for Students
Limited English proficient (LEP)	Students with a limited amount of English and who are placed in English-only classroom environments
English language learner (ELL)	Students in the process of learning English as a second language
Bilingual	Students who listen, speak, read, or write in two languages
Emergent bilingual (EB)	Students who have exposure to (listen, speak, read, or write) a heritage language while learning content in English
Multilingual learner (ML)	Students who have exposure to (listen, speak, read, or write) two or more languages while learning content in English
Culturally and linguistically diverse	Students whose homes and communities do not have Standard American English as their primary language/dialect of communication
Immigrant	Students moving to the United States from other countries
Newcomer	Students who have been in U.S. schools three years or less, particularly those at the beginning levels of English language proficiency
	Terms for Instructional Programs and Services
English as a second language (ESL) or English for speakers of other languages (ESOL)	Instructional methods or designated curricula used to teach English, with little heritage language usage; can be implemented through pull-out services or be content-based
English language development (ELD)	An instructional method focused on learning and developing language using content

(continued)

Terms for Instructional Programs and Services—(continued)	
Sheltered English instruction	An instructional method focused on making content comprehensible while supporting language development
Content-based language instruction	An instructional method similar to sheltered instruction but with an emphasis on second language acquisition principles to address students' affective, cognitive, and linguistic needs
Transitional bilingual education	A method of instruction that uses a student's heritage language in instruction and whose goal is to transition the student to an English-immersion instructional setting
Dual language programs	A two-way method of instruction whose goal is to enable students to develop proficiency in two languages

Appendix C

Instructional Routines for Structured Conversations

Turn-and-talk	Students turn to a peer and have a conversation on a topic or question posed by the teacher.
Question, stem, signal, share, assess (QSSSA) (Seidlitz & Perryman, 2021)	The teacher poses a question and provides a sentence stem. Students are given think time and signal when they're prepared to answer. Next, they share with their partner. Finally, the teacher assesses by randomly calling on students to ensure accountability and check for understanding.
Think-pair-share	Students are given time to think independently, then the teacher pairs them with another student. The student then converses with their partner to share their thinking.
Think-write-pair-share	Similar to think-pair-share, this strategy adds a writing component. Students write or draw independently as part of their thinking time.
Listen-pause-paraphrase-ask	This active listening routine begins with one student listening to their partner answer a question or share an opinion on the topic posed. The listener then pauses, paraphrases what they've heard, and asks a follow-up question. The roles then reverse so that each student has a chance to practice active listening and responding.

Appendix D

Instructional Checklists

Fostering Dialogue A checklist for embedding structured conversations	
Prior to Lesson Delivery	
Determine at what point in the lesson sequence students will respond to a question orally or engage in a structured conversation with peers.	
Craft an open-ended question.	
Determine • Who will go first (Student A, student with longest/shortest name, etc.). • Which ready signal students will give (giving a thumbs up, standing up, placing hands on head, etc.). • If the conversation will be timed.	
Consider the student's level of background knowledge. Are they familiar enough with the topic to dialogue with a peer?	
Identify vocabulary that should be used in the sentence stem/frame provided.	
During Lesson Delivery	
Pose an open-ended question.	
Give structured conversation guidelines to students that explain • Who will go first. • Which ready signal students will give.	
Recite the sentence stem. Have students repeat to practice pronunciation of vocabulary.	
Provide students with think time, and ask them to use a ready signal when they have their response.	

Appendix D

During Lesson Delivery—(continued)	
Restate the open-ended question, directing students to turn and talk.	
Check for understanding by walking around the classroom or leaning into conversations.	
Use the call-back signal to bring the class back together.	
Check for understanding and accountability by either randomly selecting a student or having students volunteer to share their or their partner's response.	

Scaffolding Writing Assignments A checklist for supporting independent writing	
Prior to Lesson Delivery	
Determine at what point in the lesson sequence students will respond to a prompt in writing.	
Craft the prompt.	
Determine the features of a written response that demonstrates mastery, considering features such as content, vocabulary, syntax, and structure.	
Consider the students' level of background knowledge. Are they familiar enough with the topic to respond in writing?	
Select the scaffolds students will need based on language proficiency: • Oral rehearsal prior to writing • Paragraph frames • Graphic organizers • Sentence stems • Word bank	
During Lesson Delivery	
Explain the writing assignment using instructional scaffolds as needed: • Use visual and verbal cues. • Clarify directions. • Model the use of scaffolds, if needed.	

Appendix E

Coaching Questions for Linguistic Growth

To Ensure Sequenced Linguistic Scaffolds	To Encourage Comprehensible Input	To Address Quality of Student Work
• What scaffolds can we include for students at the beginner or intermediate level of proficiency? • Would sentence stems or frames be more useful for this student? • How can we make this text accessible to all levels of learners? • Would the option to sketch or write enable more students to be successful? • What support could we add to this writing assignment so students at various levels can participate (word bank, graphic organizer, oral rehearsal)?	• Do students have enough background knowledge to complete this task? • What background knowledge will students need to be successful? • Which vocabulary words need to be explicitly taught? • Are there any vocabulary supports we can add for diverse learners? • Would visuals help ensure students understand this content? How? • Is the text chosen accessible to most students, including our diverse learners? Should we adapt the text or add another scaffold (visuals, highlighted vocabulary, etc.)? • What can we do for students who are reading below grade level?	• Would opportunities to speak rather than write on this assignment better enable students to show mastery? • Would an exemplar or a visual enable students to better understand the expectation? • How could paragraph frames help to enhance the quality of student writing? • What kind of feedback have we given the student? • Would the student understand the expectation better if they could watch us model a similar piece?

Appendix E

To Encourage Asset-Based Practices	To Increase the Richness of Language	To Support General Scaffolding
• What unique perspectives might the student bring, based on their cultural background? • What funds of knowledge does this student possess in general or about this learning topic? • How have we represented or reflected our student population in visual materials (images, books)? • Is there an opportunity to embed diverse students' languages or cultures into this lesson? • What opportunities for critical thinking, reflection, or feedback have been provided?	• What academic vocabulary can we include in our sentence stems? • Which tools can we use to ensure that multiple students share ideas? • Which total response signals could help us check for understanding or readiness? • How can we embed visuals into this lesson? • Which vocabulary words need to be explicitly taught? • How many opportunities will we give students to speak or orally process information during this lesson? • Which would be preferable to check for understanding: an opportunity to speak or write?	• What does mastery look like in this setting? • What is the expected outcome of this task? • What modalities (speaking, listening, reading, writing) are being used? Would one serve the goal better than another? • Which learning gap are you most concerned about? What scaffold could minimize that? • Which misconceptions in student understanding do you anticipate? Is there a scaffold that can prevent this?

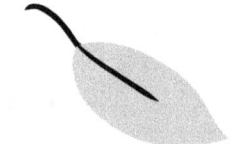
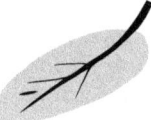

References

Aguilar, E. (2013). *The art of coaching: Effective strategies for school transformation* (1st ed.). Jossey-Bass.

Aguilar, E. (2020). *Coaching for equity: Conversations that change practice*. John Wiley & Sons.

Aguilar, E., & Cohen, L. (2022). *The PD book: 7 habits that transform professional development*. Wiley.

Angelou, M. (1995, January). Celebrities. *Jet Magazine*.

Bandura, A. (1997). *Self-efficacy: The exercise of control* (1st ed.). Worth Publishers.

Billak, B. (2019, February 19). Push-in and pull-out: Understanding ESL services. *The International Educator (TIE Online)*. https://www.tieonline.com/article/1537/push-in-and-pull-out-understanding-esl-services#:~:text=The%20goal%20is%20to%20develop,going%20on%20at%20that%20time.

Brackett, M. (2020). *Permission to feel: The power of emotional intelligence to achieve well-being and success*. Celadon Books.

Brackett, M., Delaney, S., & Salovey, P. (2025). Emotional intelligence. In R. Biswas-Diener & E. Diener (Eds.), *Noba textbook series: Psychology*. DEF publishers. http://noba.to/xzvpfun7

Brown, B. (2018). *Dare to lead: Brave work. Tough conversations. Whole hearts*. Random House.

Cárdenas-Hagan, E. (2020). *Literacy foundations for English learners: A comprehensive guide to evidence-based instruction*. Paul H. Brookes Publishing.

CASEL. (2023, March). What is the CASEL framework? https://casel.org/fundamentals-of-sel/what-is-the-casel-framework/#self-management

Center on Multi-Tiered System of Supports. (n.d.) Progress monitoring. https://mtss4success.org/essential-components/progress-monitoring

Cheliotes, L. M. G., & Reilly, M. F. (2018). *Coaching conversations: Transforming your school one conversation at a time*. Corwin.

Chenoweth, R. (2019, September 5). *Rudine Sims Bishop: "Mother" of multicultural children's literature*. College of Education and Human Ecology. https://ehe.osu.edu/news/listing/rudine-sims-bishop-diverse-childrens-books

References

Clear, J. (2020, April 13). The beginner's guide to deliberate practice. https://jamesclear.com/beginners-guide-deliberate-practice

Cooper, A. (2020). *And justice for ELs: A leader's guide to creating and sustaining equitable schools.* Corwin.

Corwin Visible Learning Plus. (n.d.). Feedback. https://www.visiblelearningmetax.com/influences/view/feedback

DiClemente, J. O., & Prochaska. C. C. (1983). Stages and processes of self-change of smoking: Toward an integrative model of change. *Journal of Consulting and Clinical Psychology, 51*(3), 390–395

Dove, M. G., & Honigsfeld, A. (2017). *Co-teaching for English learners: A guide to collaborative planning, instruction, assessment, and reflection.* Corwin.

DuFour, R., DuFour, R. B., Eaker, R. E., Many, T. W., & Mattos, M. W. (2016). *Learning by doing: A handbook for professional learning communities at work* (3rd ed.). Solution Tree.

Fenner, D. S., & Snyder, S. (2017). *Unlocking English learners' potential: Strategies for Making Content Accessible.* Corwin.

Fenner, D. S., & Teich, M. (2024). *Social emotional learning for multilingual learners: Essential actions for success.*

Garcia, A. (2021, June 18). Words matter: The case for shifting to "emergent bilingual." *Language Magazine.* https://www.languagemagazine.com/2021/06/17/words-matter-the-case-for-shifting-to-emergent-bilingual/

Gibbons, K., Brown, S., & Niebling, B. C. (2018). *Effective universal instruction: An action-oriented approach to improving Tier 1.* Guilford Press.

Goodwin, B., Rouleau, K., Abla, C., Baptiste, K., Gibson, T., & Kimball, M. (2022). *The new classroom instruction that works: The best research-based strategies for increasing student achievement.* ASCD.

Hammond, Z. (2014). *Culturally responsive teaching and the brain: Promoting authentic engagement and rigor among culturally and linguistically diverse students.* Corwin.

Heath, C., & Heath, D. (2010). *Switch: How to change things when change is hard.* Broadway Books.

Huynh, T. (2021, August 26). #49. Instructional program models for teaching English: ELL strategies. https://tankhuynh.com/instructional-program-models/

Instructional Design Australia. (2024, March 13). Andragogy: Adult learning theory. https://instructionaldesign.com.au/andragogy-adult-learning-theory/

Kee, K., Anderson, K., Dearing, V., Shuster, F., & National Staff Development Council (U.S.). (2010). *RESULTS coaching: The new essential for school leaders.* Sage Publications.

Khalifeh, G. B. (2023, November 7). How high achievers can avoid the arrival fallacy. LinkedIn. https://www.linkedin.com/pulse/how-high-achievers-can-avoid-arrival-fallacy-ghada-p1avf/

Knight, J. (2015). *Better conversations: Coaching ourselves and each other to be more credible, caring, and connected.* Sage Publications.

Knight, J. (2017). *The impact cycle: What instructional coaches should do to foster powerful improvements in teaching.* Sage Publications.

Knight, J. (2022). *The definitive guide to instructional coaching: Seven factors for success.* ASCD.

Kongsvik, J. (n.d.). The four domains of language: Listening. TESOL Trainers. https://tesol-trainers.com/siop/siop-practice-and-application/siop-feature-22/the-four-domains-of-language-listening

Krashen, S. D. (1982). *Principles and practice in second language acquisition*. Pergamon Press. https://www.sdkrashen.com/content/books/principles_and_practice.pdf

Lau v. Nichols, 414 U.S. 563 (1974).

Lee, M. (2024, June 28). What you need to know: Six principles of adult learning. Confianza. https://ellstudents.com/blogs/the-confianza-way/what-you-need-to-know-six-principles-of-andragogy

Marzano, R. J. (2017). *The new art and science of teaching*. Solution Tree.

Marzano, R. J. (2019). *The handbook for* The New Art and Science of Teaching. Solution Tree.

Marzano, R. J., Rains, C. L., & Warrick, P. B. (2020). *Improving teacher development and evaluation: A guide for leaders, coaches, and teachers*. Marzano Resources.

Maxwell, J. C. (2011). *The 360 degree leader: Developing your influence from anywhere in the organization*. HarperCollins Leadership.

Moats, L. C. (2020). *Speech to print: Language essentials for teachers*. Brookes Publishing.

Mohamed, N. (2023, July 11). *Terminology matters: What do you call your (English) learners?* | TESOL.

National Center for Education Statistics (NCES). (2024, May). English learners in public schools. U.S. Department of Education, Institute of Education Sciences. https://nces.ed.gov/programs/coe/indicator/cgf.

National Clearinghouse for English Language Acquisition (NCELA). (n.d.). English learners: Demographic trends (August 2022). https://ncela.ed.gov/resources/fact-sheet-english-learners-demographic-trends-august-2022-0

Neff, K. (2011). *Self-compassion: The proven power of being kind to yourself*. Harper Collins.

Phelan, H. (2018, December 20). What's all this about journaling? *New York Times*. https://www.nytimes.com/2018/10/25/style/journaling-benefits.html

Pierson, R. (2013, May). Every kid needs a champion. [Video]. TED Talk. https://www.ted.com/talks/rita_pierson_every_kid_needs_a_champion?subtitle=en

Porosoff, L. (2023). *Teach for authentic engagement*. ASCD.

The Reading League. (2022). *Science of reading: Defining guide*. https://thereadingleague.org/wp-content/uploads/2022/03/Science-of-Reading-eBook-2022.pdf

Sedita, J. (2023). *The writing rope: A framework for explicit writing instruction in all subjects*. Brookes Publishing.

Seidlitz, J., & Perryman, B. (2021). *7 steps to a language-rich interactive classroom: Research-based strategies for engaging all students* (2nd ed.). Seidlitz Education.

Snyder, S., & Fenner, D. S. (2021). *Culturally responsive teaching for multilingual learners: Tools for equity*. Corwin.

Solution Tree. (2023). History of PLC. All Things PLC. https://allthingsplc.info/about/history-of-plc/

Spangler, D. (2022, October 6). Using video as a coaching tool with first-year teachers. *Edutopia*. https://www.edutopia.org/article/using-video-coaching-tool-first-year-teacher

Sparks, S. D. (2024, April 4). Why teacher-student relationships matter. *Education Week*. https://www.edweek.org/teaching-learning/why-teacher-student-relationships-matter/2019/03

Strategies for Influence. (n.d.). Peter Senge: Learning organizations. https://strategiesforinfluence.com/peter-senge-learning-organization/

Sweeney, D. (2010). *Student-centered coaching: A guide for K–8 coaches and principals*. Corwin.

Sweeney, D., & Harris, L. S. (2020). *The essential guide for student-centered coaching: What every K–12 coach and school leader needs to know*. Corwin.

Sweeney, D., & Mausbach, A. (2018). *Leading student-centered coaching: Building principal and coach partnerships*. Corwin.

Tomlinson, C. A. (n.d.). What is differentiated instruction? Reading Rockets. https://www.readingrockets.org/topics/differentiated-instruction/articles/what-differentiated-instruction

Tuckman, B. W. (1965). Developmental sequence in small groups. *Psychological Bulletin, 63*(6), 384–399.

U.S. Department of Education. (n.d.). Developing ELL programs: Glossary. https://web.archive.org/web/20240821002624/https://www2.ed.gov/about/offices/list/ocr/ell/glossary.html

U.S. Department of Justice. (2021, March 25). *Types of educational opportunities discrimination*. Civil Rights Division. https://www.justice.gov/crt/types-educational-opportunities-discrimination

U.S. Department of Justice & U.S. Department of Education. (2015). Dear colleague letter: English learner students and limited English proficient parents. https://www2.ed.gov/about/offices/list/ocr/letters/colleague-el-201501.pdf

Waack, S. (2018, October 12). Collective teacher efficacy (CTE) according to John Hattie. Visible Learning. https://visible-learning.org/2018/03/collective-teacher-efficacy-hattie/#:~:text=Collective%20Teacher%20Efficacy%20is%20the,strongly%20correlated%20with%20student%20achievement.

Wiggins, G. (2021). Seven keys to effective feedback. *Educational Leadership, 70*(1). https://www.ascd.org/el/articles/seven-keys-to-effective-feedback

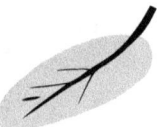

Index

The letter *f* following a page locator denotes a figure.

access gap, 32
accommodations
    academic, 32
    aligning, 38
    linguistic, 32–39, 35*f*
    targeted, 38–39
adjourning teaming stage, 99
adult learning, principles of, 15
arrival fallacy, 136
assessment
    formative, 53
    Inclusion with a Purpose model, 87–88
    for progress monitoring, 52–54
    self-rating, 58–60
audio review, 62–63

beliefs, asset-based, 22–26
bias, monolingual, 26
bids for connection, 46
bilingual, 145
bilingual education, transitional, 146

celebration
    Goal Setting model, 76–78
    Inclusion with a Purpose model, 87–88

change
    embracing, 137
    stages of, 138*f*
checklists
    Coaching Minicycles model, 114–115
    for embedding structured conversations, 148–149
    for supporting independent writing, 149
classroom environments, language- and literacy-rich, 27–32
classroom management, 31
coaches
    leading from the middle, 56
    time commitments by level, 56, 57*f*
coaching
    background of, 1–2
    benefits of, 2
    collaborative, 45*f*, 56–63, 57*f*
    consultative, 45*f*, 46–49
    goal of, 68, 131
    language acquisition, 2–3
    levels of, 45*f*
    matching to a team's stage, 94–99
    reflective, 45*f*, 49–55
    self-awareness as foundational to, 8

coaching core beliefs
  collective efficacy, 9f, 11–12
  communication, 9f, 16–17
  continuous improvement, 9f, 12–13
  emotional intelligence, 9–11, 9f, 12
  lifelong learning, 9f, 13–14
  partnership, 9f, 15
Coaching Mini-cycle coaching model, 68f, 109–119
coaching models
  implementation considerations, 132–133
  inclusive vs. exclusive, 44
  overview, 67, 68f
coaching models, student-centered
  Goal Setting, 68f, 70–78
  Inclusion with a Purpose, 15, 53, 68f, 79–88
  program models vs., 80–81, 81f
  teacher-centered models vs., 68–70, 69f
coaching models, teacher-centered
  Coaching Minicycles, 68f, 109–119
  Collaborative Planning. *see* Collaborative Planning coaching model
  Co-Teaching Cycle, 15, 53, 68f, 120–132
  student-centered models vs., 68–70, 68f
co-delivery
  Coaching Minicycles model, 115–116
  Co-Teaching Cycle model, 128, 130
collaboration, 10, 12, 93–94
Collaborative Planning coaching model
  coach's role in, 92–94
  overview, 68f
  preparations, 105–106
  reflection coaching moves, 100–104, 100f
  resourcing coaching moves, 100f, 104–105
  teaming stages, 95–99, 95f
collaborative teaming stage, 95f
collective teacher efficacy (CTE), defined, 11–12

communication
  committed listening in, 47, 142
  core belief of coaching, 9f, 16–17
  paraphrasing in, 50, 101–102, 118–119, 143
conferences
  Coaching Minicycles model, 110–114
  Co-Teaching Cycle model, 123–127, 125f
  Goal Setting model, 72–73
  Inclusion with a Purpose model, 83–85, 85f
consultative teaming stage, 95f
continuous improvement, a core belief, 9f, 12–13
conversations
  collaborative, 12
  dialogue, fostering, 148
  in engagement, 31–32
  life-giving, 110, 119
  productive, 117
  reflective structures, 132f
  structured, 32, 35, 60, 147–149
co-planning
  Coaching Minicycles model, 114–115
  as a coaching move, 54
  Co-Teaching Cycle model, 127–128
Co-Teaching Cycle coaching model, 15, 53, 68f, 120–132

data collection for progress monitoring, 52–54
differentiation, 36–38, 37f
diversity, cultural and linguistic, 143
dual language programs, 146

early intermediate level, descriptor, 37f
education, transitional bilingual, 146
efficacy, collective, 9f, 11–12
efficacy beliefs, 38
emergent bilingual (EB), 145
emergent level, descriptor, 37f
emotional intelligence, 9–12, 9f, 62
empower, 25–26

engagement, 25–26, 30–32
English as a second language (ESL), 145
English for speakers of other languages (ESOL), 145
English instruction, sheltered, 146
English language, 29
English language development (ELD), 145
English Language learner (ELL), 145
English learner (EL), 20, 44
environments, language- and literacy-rich, 27–32
Equal Education Opportunities Act (EEOA), 2

feedback, 51, 116–119
filters, affective, 33–35, 34*f*
forming teaming stage, 95–96, 95*f*

glossaries, linguistic, 33
goal setting, 58, 121–122
Goal Setting coaching model, 68*f*, 70–78
good, witnessing the, 11, 48
grace in building trust, 47–48

happiness, achieving, 136–137
heart work, 10

immigrant, 143
Inclusion with a Purpose coaching model, 15, 53, 68*f*, 79–88
information, sharing to improve instruction, 49
instruction. *See also* language acquisition instruction
    comprehensible, 33–36, 36*f*
    content-based language, 146
    differentiated, 36–38, 37*f*
    linguistically accommodated, 32–39
    modeling lessons, 52
    segregated instructional model, 2
    sharing information to improve, 49
    sheltered English, 146

instructional coaching. *See* coaching
instructional strategies, affirming, 100–101
integrity in building trust, 47
intermediate level, descriptor, 37*f*

journaling, 61–62

language acquisition coaching, 2–3
language acquisition instruction, layers of quality
    asset-based practices, 22–26
    equity-driven practices, 22–26
    focus of, 22
    four-step process, 39–40, 40*f*
    language- and literacy-rich environment, 27–32
    linguistically accommodated instruction, 32–39
    overview, 22*f*
leading from the middle, 56
learning
    principles of adult, 15
    professional, 13–14
lessons, modeling, 52
lifelong learning, 9*f*, 13–14
Limited English proficient (LEP), 145
Limited English speaking ability (LESA), 20
linguistic growth, coaching questions for, 150–151
listening
    committed, 47, 142
    foundational skill of, 27
    quiet, 119
Listen-pause-paraphrase-ask, 147
literacy, 28–30, 31

mindset
    asset-based vs. deficit-based, 22–24, 23*f*
    a coaching, 14
    defined, 12
Mini-cycle coaching model, 68*f*, 109–119

modeling strategies, 104–105
motivation, 9–10
moves, 15
multilingual learners (ML), 145

near proficient level, descriptor, 37*f*
newcomer kits, 16
newcomers, 37*f*, 145
norming teaming stage, 95*f*, 97

oracy, 27–28
oral language skills, 27–30
orthography, 29

paraphrasing, 50, 101–102, 118–119, 143
partnerships
    collaborative, 12
    communication and, 16–17
    core belief of coaching, 9*f*, 15
    Co-Teaching Cycle, 120–132
    full, 15
performing teaming stage, 95*f*, 98
phonological awareness, 28
practitioner goals, setting, 58
professional learning communities (PLCs), 92
proficiency levels with descriptors, 37*f*
progress monitoring, 52–54

Question, stem, signal, share, assess (QSSSA), 147
questioning
    Co-Teaching Cycle conferences, 125*f*
    for linguistic growth, 150–151
    powerful, 144
    reflective, 50, 117
    role in Collaborative Planning, 102–104

reading, foundational skill of, 28–30
reflection. *See also* self-reflection
    Coaching Minicycles model, 109, 116–119
    Co-Teaching Cycle model, 130–131, 132*f*

reflection—(*continued*)
    Goal Setting model, 76–78
    Inclusion with a Purpose model, 87–88
    role in Collaborative Planning, 100–104, 100*f*
reflective teaming stage, 95*f*
rehearsing, 62
relationships
    bids for connection, 46
    in classroom management, 31
    in consultative coaching, 46–47
    importance of, 24–25
    listening in, 47
    trust in, 47–48
relevance, 25–26
resourcing role in Collaborative Planning, 100*f*, 104–105
rigor, 26

safety
    creating, 93
    through paraphrasing, 50
scaffolds
    history courses, 93
    Inclusion with a Purpose model, 79, 86
    instructional, 33
    linguistic, 26, 32
    material, 33
    by proficiency, 37*f*
    suggesting in Collaborative planning, 104
    targeted, 38–39
    writing assignments, 149
self-awareness, 8, 13, 59, 61
self-care, 61–62
self-rating, 58–60
self-reflection, 59–60, 63, 109. *See also* reflection
self-reflection scales, 60
servant leadership, 47, 104
speaking, foundational skill of, 27
storming teaming stage, 95*f*, 96–97

students
- culturally and linguistically diverse, defined, 21
- English proficient, 22
- goal-setting for, 55
- reclassifying as English proficient, 22

students, multilingual
- advocating for, 46
- defined, 20, 21
- goals for, 22, 38, 67
- progress monitoring, 52–54
- pull-out services, 79–80
- push-in services, 79
- responsibility toward, 22
- rights of, 32–33

success, defining, 13, 122

syntactic awareness, 30

theory vs. practice, 66

thinking collaboratively, 50, 54

Think-pair-share, 147

Think-write-pair-share, 147

transfer, 109, 120–121

trust, building and maintaining, 47–48

Turn-and-talk, 147

video review, 62–63

vision, developing a, 9–10

windows, mirrors, and sliding glass doors, 25

witnessing the good, 11, 48

worthiness, affirming, 24

writing
- checklist for supporting independent, 149
- foundational skill of, 28–30

About the Author

Paula Polk has served in education for 16 years, teaching 1st grade and 3rd grade for the first 10 years of her educational career. Her journey into educational leadership began as a language coach; she then embarked into district leadership as an English as a second language (ESL) facilitator. In this role, she coaches language coaches, language acquisition specialists, and ESL teachers preK–12 as they work with stakeholders, including administrators, teachers, and multilingual students and families. This role also affords her the opportunity to curate professional learning for teachers, coaches, district coordinators, and administrators as they seek to create spaces for multilingual students to thrive. You can learn more about her work at https://coachreflective.org.

Related ASCD Resources

At the time of publication, the following resources were available (ASCD stock numbers in parentheses).

Centering ELLs in the Science of Reading (Quick Reference Guide) by Aileen Hower and Pérsida Himmele (#QRG124087)

The Consciously Unbiased Educator by Huda Essa (#121014)

Dispelling Misconceptions About English Language Learners: Research-Based Ways to Improve Instruction by Barbara Gottschalk (#120010)

From Stressed Out to Stress Wise: How You and Your Students Can Navigate Challenges and Nurture Vitality by Abby Wills, Anjali Deva, and Niki Saccareccia (#123004)

Learning in a New Language: A Schoolwide Approach to Support K–8 Emergent Bilinguals by Lori Helman (#120015)

Learning Unlimited: Strategies for Students with Limited or Interrupted Formal Education and Other Struggling Multilingual Learners by Nicoleta Filimon and Christi Cartwright-Lacerda (#124010)

Planning Effective Instruction for ELLs (Quick Reference Guide) by Pérsida Himmele and William Himmele (#QRG119029)

Success with Multicultural Newcomers & English Learners: Proven Practices for School Leadership Teams by Margarita Espino Calderón and Shawn Slakk (#117026)

For up-to-date information about ASCD resources, go to www.ascd.org. You can search the complete archives of *Educational Leadership* at www.ascd.org/el. To contact us, send an email to member@ascd.org or call 1-800-933-2723 or 703-578-9600.

Transform Instruction to
Transform Students' Lives

Our Transformational Learning Principles (TLPs) are evidence-based practices that ensure students have access to high-impact, joyful learning experiences.

Endorsed by AASA and NASSP, the TLPs provide a shared language and a framework for reimagining teaching and learning, focusing on nurturing student growth, guiding intellectual curiosity, and empowering learners to take ownership of their education.

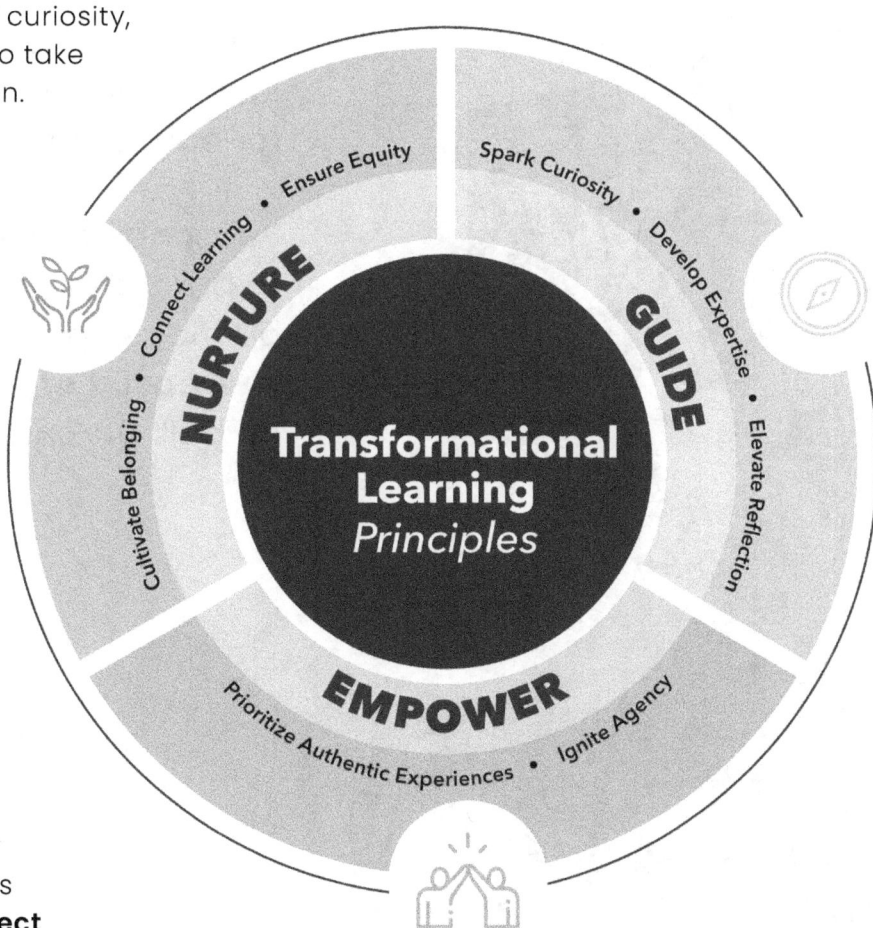

Enhancing Instruction for Multilingual Learners relates to the **ensure equity, connect learning to the learner,** and **ignite agency** principles.

Learn more at **ascd.org/tlps**

DON'T MISS A SINGLE ISSUE OF THIS AWARD-WINNING MAGAZINE.

iste+ascd
educational leadership

If you belong to a Professional Learning Community, you may be looking for a way to get your fellow educators' minds around a complex topic. Why not delve into a relevant theme issue of *Educational Leadership*, the journal written by educators for educators?

Subscribe now and browse or purchase back issues of our flagship publication at **www.ascd.org/el**. Discounts on bulk purchases are available.

iste+ascd

Arlington, VA USA
1-800-933-2723

www.ascd.org
www.iste.org

www.ingramcontent.com/pod-product-compliance
Lightning Source LLC
Chambersburg PA
CBHW060538010526
44119CB00052B/750